PRESSURE COOKER COOKBOOK

Best Instant Pot Receipes for Beginners and Advanced Users

(The Most Wanted Electric Pressure Cooker Cookbook)

Crystal Ruggles

Published by Sharon Lohan

© **Crystal Ruggles**

All Rights Reserved

Pressure Cooker Cookbook: Best Instant Pot Receipes for Beginners and Advanced Users (The Most Wanted Electric Pressure Cooker Cookbook)

ISBN 978-1-990334-26-9

All rights reserved. No part of this guide may be reproduced in any form without permission in writing from the publisher except in the case of brief quotations embodied in critical articles or reviews.

Legal & Disclaimer

The information contained in this book is not designed to replace or take the place of any form of medicine or professional medical advice. The information in this book has been provided for educational and entertainment purposes only.

The information contained in this book has been compiled from sources deemed reliable, and it is accurate to the best of the Author's knowledge; however, the Author cannot guarantee its accuracy and validity and cannot be held liable for any errors or omissions. Changes are periodically made to this book. You must consult your doctor or get professional medical advice before using any of the suggested remedies, techniques, or information in this book.

Table of contents

Part 1 1
Introduction 2
Chapter 1: Pressure Cooking Explained 3
Chapter 2: Pressure Cooking Benefits 5
Chapter 3: Pressure Cooking Tips to Keep in Mind 8
Chapter 4: Pressure Cooker Recipes: Meat Dishes 11
Beef Dishes 11
Pressure Cooker Corned Beef 11
Chili con Carne 13
Beef Pot Roast 14
Pasta Casserole 15
Boneless Pork Roast w/ Fennel 18
Pork Loin w/ Veggies 19
Char Siu (Chinese-Style Pork Barbecue) 21
Lamb Dishes 23
Lamb Shanks 23
Lamb Barley Stew 24
Chapter 5: Pressure Cooker Recipes – Fish and Seafood Dishes 27
Fish Chowder 27
Mediterranean Style Fish 28
Octopus and Potatoes 29
Salmon Al Cartoccio 32
Coconut Fish Curry 33
Chapter 6: Pressure Cooker Recipes – Vegetarian Dishes 36

Pumpkin Soup 36
Vegetarian Chili 37
Lemoned Broccoli 39
Risotto with Artichoke Hearts 40
Vegetable Curry 42
Conclusion 44
Part 2 45
Introduction 46
Chapter 1: Creating Clean And Healthy Meals With The Electric Pressure Cooker 47
Chapter 2: Benefits Of Electric Pressure Cooking 57
Chapter 3: Necessary Tools To Get You Started 60
Chapter 4: Tips For Planning Your Meals Ahead Of Time 65
Chapter 5: Common Mistakes To Avoid 70
Chapter 6: Easy Pressure Cooker Breakfast Recipes 73
Recipe #1 : Apple, Berry and Nuts Risotto 74
Recipe #2 : Gluten-Free Egg Muffins 76
Recipe #3 : Potatoes and Sweet Potatoes Hash Browns 78
Recipe #4 : Quinoa with Brown Rice "Cereal" 80
Recipe #5 : Tea Eggs 82
Recipe #6 : Raisin Bread Pudding with Salted Caramel 84
Recipe #7 : Fluffy Scrambled Eggs 87
Recipe #8 : Hungarian Sausage Omelet 89
Recipe #9 : Easy Mushroom Soup in the Morning 91
Recipe #10 : Breakfast Chocolate Drink (Kiddie Version) 92
Recipe #11 : Breakfast Chocolate Drink (Adult Version) 93
Recipe #12 : Pot Torte with Frozen Fruit Sauce 94

Recipe #13 : Cheesy Cauliflower Pops 97

Recipe #14 : Faux Pho 98

Recipe #15 : Breadless Sausage Burger 101

Recipe #16 : Easy Cheesy Chicken Salad 103

Recipe #17 : Corned Beef Hash 106

Recipe #18 : Smoked Salmon on Scrambled Eggs 108

Recipe #19 : French Toast Pudding with Choco Hazelnut ... 110

Recipe #20 : French Toast Pudding with Nuts and Jam 112

Recipe #21 : Pasta Pasticciata (A Mess of Pasta) 114

Recipe #22 : Creamy One Pot Chicken and Vegetable Soup 116

Recipe #23 : Easy Mushroom Stew 117

Recipe #24 : Spicy Butternut Squash Soup 119

Recipe #25 : Meaty Grain Stew with Spinach 122

Recipe #26 : Chickpea, Potato and Spinach Soup 124

Recipe #27 : Green Soup (Pea and Potato Soup) 126

Recipe #28 : Quick Clam Chowder 128

Recipe #29 : Easy Onion Soup 130

Recipe #30 : Pea Soup in a Flash 132

Recipe #31 : Chunky Tomato Soup with Tortilla Chips 134

Recipe #32 : Shrimp and Pea Stew 136

Recipe #33 : Squash Soup 138

Recipe #35 : 10 Vegetables in a Soup 141

Recipe #36 : No Fuss Chicken Soup 144

Recipe #37 : Sour Shrimp with Daikon and Water Spinach 146

Recipe #38 : Sour Pork with Daikon and Taro 148

Recipe #39 : Vegetable Curry in Lemongrass Coconut Sauce 150

Recipe #40 : Spicy Italian Sausage Stew 153
Recipe #41 : Meaty Beef Broth 155
Recipe #42 : Meaty Pork Broth 156
Recipe #43 : Meaty Chicken Broth 158
Recipe #44 : Easy Fish Broth With Herbs 160
Recipe #45 : Grouper in Ginger Soup with Cabbage 162
Recipe #46 : Quick, Easy, Chewy Miso Soup 163
Recipe #47 : Spicy Beef Sandwich 166
Recipe #48 : Pulled Pork Sandwich in a Pot 168
Recipe #49 : Fresh Tuna Salad Sandwich with Lemon Mayo 171
Recipe #50 : Chicken Liver with Spicy Herbed Rice 173
Recipe #51 : Beef Stew with Parsnips 176
Recipe #52 : Beef Stew with Peanut Sauce and Vegetables 178
Recipe #53 : Beef Stew with Tomato-Peanut Sauce 180
Recipe #53 : Seafood Laksa 182
Recipe #54 : Chicken Laksa with Ho-fun Noodles 185
Recipe #55 : Chicken in Coconut Ginger Sauce 187
Recipe #56 : Chicken and Cauliflower Stew 189
Conclusion 192

Part 1

Introduction

This book contains simple and easy to prepare recipes cooked using a pressure cooker that the whole family will enjoy.

Pressure-cooked food has a lot of health benefits. For one, the nutrients and flavor of the food are retained. In addition, it is deemed as one of the most energy-efficient methods of cooking. This is because pressure cooking cuts the time required to cook using conventional methods by as much as 70%.

This is ideal for working people who need to rush home from work to prepare freshly cooked meals for the family. What's more, after the dish is done, clean up is a breeze. After all, there is only one pot to clean.

Aside from the recipes, you will also learn various tips on how to get the best results when cooking meals using the pressure cooker. Once you learn the basics, you are ready to experiment and whip up your own recipes based on your particular taste and preferences.

Let's begin the journey.

Chapter 1: Pressure Cooking Explained

What Is Pressure Cooking?

An energy-saving method of cooking that does the job more quickly than traditional methods, pressure cooking uses a sealed container (pressure cooker) with water or other cooking liquids. The process does not allow liquids or air to escape under a pre-set pressure level.

Pressure cookers are able to quickly heat food because of the internal steam pressure that comes from the boiling water or liquid. This causes wet or saturated steam to permeate and bombard the food being cooked. The higher temperature of the water vapor allows faster transfer of heat (compared to dry air), and faster cooking. This reduces the amount of energy required to cook a particular dish because the water is not made to boil for a long time.

Upon reaching the target temperature, heat is lost only through the cooker's surface. Thus, pressure cooking is considered as the most efficient cooking method in terms of energy-efficiency.

Parts of a Pressure Cooker

Pressure cookers are usually made of stainless steel or aluminum. Aluminum models may be anodized, polished, or stamped, and are generally not dish-washer safe. They are also reactive to acidic foods, thus possibly altering the flavor of the dish being cooked. They are cheaper, and expectedly less durable than steel models.

Almost all portable pressure cookers today have the following parts and components, depending on the particular model and manufacturer:

Pan

- Metal body
- Pan Handle/s; some models have one handle; others have two, one on each side

Lid

- Lid handle, typically equipped with a locking mechanism (button or slider) that locks the cooker and prevents the lid from being removed while in use
- Sealing ring or gasket that seals the pressure cooker airtight
- Steam vent fitted with a pressure regulator at the top (either a spring device or weight) that maintains the pan's pressure level.
- Pressure indicator pin that indicates the absence or presence of pressure, no matter how slight
- Safety devices typically release valves for over pressure/over temperature pressure
- Pressure gauge that is normally seen in high-end models

Accessories – These usually include a steamer basket, a trivet to keep the steamer basket over the cooking liquid, and a metal divider that is used to separate food varieties in the steamer such as vegetables.

Chapter 2: Pressure Cooking Benefits

Pressure cookers have been used all over the world for a long time, although some people are still reluctant to use one. The hesitation may be due to some unpleasant childhood memories when using a pressure cooker came with some risks. In the past, aside from the screeching pressure cooker sound while in use, some models had the tendency to explode, sending the family's dinner to smithereens, splattered all over the kitchen and the ceiling.

Safety Features of Present-Day Pressure Cookers

The pressure cookers today are very safe to use and there is almost 0% possibility of exploding. Today's models also do not create the high-pitched, scary screeching sounds that came with the old versions. In addition, current pressure cookers are equipped with safety features that prevent buildup of excess pressure. Likewise, lid handle locks are designed not to open unless the pressure is released first. Simply put, present models are a far cry from the noisy, rattling, and steam-spewing pots that our grandparents are familiar with.

Pressure Cooking Benefits

A pressure cooker is a fixture in many kitchens today. It makes food preparation easier, and saves a lot of energy and time. Following are some of the major benefits you can expect from pressure cooking.

Food is tastier and retains most of the nutrients. – Food cooked using a pressure cooker offers more nutritional benefits than dishes cooked using traditional cooking methods for a longer period of time. This is because more nutrients are lost the longer a particular dish is cooked. On the other hand, it takes a significantly shorter amount of time to pressure cook, with less liquid or water used. Once the liquid is boiled away, the food is left with most of its nutrients intact.

Using a pressure cooker reduces typical cooking time by up to 70%. Traditional cooking methods require boiling food for a long time, and this causes the natural flavor of the ingredients to be steamed away. On the other hand, pressure cooking improves the natural flavor and richness of foods.

It saves a significant amount of energy. – One pressure cooker can do the job of several pots used on separate burners, and this translates to a considerable amount of energy savings. Many recipes can be cooked using the pressure cooker alone, and because various dishes are cooked much more quickly, less energy is used for cooking. With today's ever increasing cost of power, this is one great way to cut down on utility consumption.

It significantly cuts meal preparation time. – Pressure cooking reduces cooking time by as much as 70%. You can quickly whip up a delicious meal to feed a hungry family. Gone are the days when you get home from work with little energy left to cook, but you need to quickly put dinner on the table. A one-pot meal can easily be prepared with a pressure cooker. Your nutritious and delicious dinner will be ready in a matter of minutes. Just toss in the ingredients and by the time you finish setting up the table, dinner is ready to be served.

You enjoy a cooler kitchen. – With the record-setting number of heat waves sweeping most parts of the country in summer, having a cool kitchen is quite a relief. Cooking with traditional stove-top pans and pots produces heat that travels upwards. While some of the heat is sent out of the house through the stovetop fan, heat in the kitchen builds up as well. A pressure cooker, on the other hand, retains the steam and heat inside the cooker, allowing nothing to escape that can heat up the kitchen. This results to a cooler kitchen.

It requires less cleaning. – When cooking using traditional stove-top pots, you cannot help but leave residues on the control panel and stove-top, and at times, even on adjacent surfaces like counters and walls. This is due to the escaping steam and oils from the open cookware. All these require some time to clean up once the dish is done. On the other hand, a pressure cooker is safely secured with a lid that keeps unnecessary spatters and splashes from escaping the cooker. Likewise, the lid gets rid of possible boil overs that require additional cleaning. When the entire meal is done, you only have to wash one pot.

It can also be used for preserving food. – Pressure cooking can also be used to prepare foods intended for canning and to be kept for future consumption. This is why bigger models are also called "canners." These models can usually build pressure up to 15 psi, the required high pressure for cooking and canning of various foods like fish and meat. Smaller models can be utilized for home canning purposes as they hold a significantly lower amount than commercial models.

Chapter 3: Pressure Cooking Tips to Keep in Mind

After learning the benefits of pressure cooking and how it works, it is time to learn a few important adjustments you need to make on the traditional cooking methods you have gotten used to in order to optimize your use of the pressure cooker. Follow these tips and you are guaranteed to enjoy great pressure cooking results.

Put brown meats, poultry and veggies (such as carrots, peppers or chopped onions) first; then deglaze the cooker for more natural flavor. - Simply add some oil like canola or olive oil to the cooker without the lid, and heat over medium-high heat. Add small batches of food and cook until the food is brown all over. Transfer the food to a bowl and set it aside. Loosen up and take the tasty cooked-on juices and small food particles left by deglazing the cooker pot using a small amount of broth, wine, or even just plain water. Replace the cooked food inside the pot together with the rest of the ingredients. Allow to cook under pressure.

Evenly-sized pieces of food means food that is evenly cooked. – Cut the raw food into uniform-sized portions to make sore that they all cook evenly in a given amount of time.

Begin at high, and finish at low. – Begin pressure cooking at high heat. Once you reach the target pressure, bring the burner down to a simmer. You do not have to worry about heat adjustments when using an electric pressure cooker as it automatically does it for you.

Avoid overdoing the liquid. – Because the food is cooked under pressure in a sealed pot, there is less evaporation. It follows that less cooking is liquid compared to cooking using conventional means. It is important, however, to make sure that there is enough liquid, regardless of the dish you are preparing. 1 cup of liquid is usually a good rule of thumb to follow, but to be sure, check the user's manual or refer to the recipe book to find out exactly how much liquid the product manufacturer recommends. Never, under any circumstances, fill the cooker with liquid in excess of half of its full capacity.

Never load the cooker with an excessive amount of food. – Do not fill up over 2/3 of the pressure cooker capacity with food or ingredients. Likewise do not tightly pack food in the cooker. Ignoring this all-important pressure cooking guideline may result to the inefficient operation of your pressure cooker, possibly affecting the quality of the finished product. It may also trigger the activation of he built-in safety mechanisms of the cooker, particularly if there is a large amount of food in the cooker.

For best results, use the stop-and-go cooking method. – When doing a recipe that has ingredients requiring varying cooking times, start by putting slow to cook ingredients like meats first. To stop cooking, apply the quick-release method. Add the easy to cook ingredients like peas or green beans next. Bring the pressure back up and finish cooking the entire dish at the same time.

Avoid burning when using a stove-top pressure cooker by playing burner hopscotch. – Upon reaching pressure at high heat, adjust the burner down to a simmer. Most gas burner models quickly react, but not most electric models. If you are using an electric stove, you can use 2 burners, one at high heat to achieve pressure and the other at low setting for maintaining pressure. Switch to the low setting burner once pressure is reached.

Set the timer. – Keep a kitchen timer within reach so that once the cooker achieves and maintains the target pressure, you can easily set it for the recipe-specified cooking time. Some electric pressure cooker models have a built-in digital timer.

It may take a longer time to cook at high altitude. – If you live in a high-altitude area, you may need to adjust your cooking time, especially if you are at 3,000 ft. above sea level, at least. Follow the generally-accepted rule of thumb, which is to increase cooking times by 5% for every 1000 ft. in excess of 2,000 ft. above sea level.

Release the pressure. – When you are done pressure cooking, use the appropriate method to release pressure, depending on the recipe you are working on.

Chapter 4: Pressure Cooker Recipes: Meat Dishes

Beef Dishes

Pressure Cooker Corned Beef

An all-time family favorite, corned beef is simple and quite easy to prepare, more so when pressure cooked. It will also remain good for a long period of time when refrigerated. In addition, leftovers can be recycled to make tasty sandwiches, or served with other dishes next time.

Makes 6 servings

Preparation Time: 1 hour

Cooking Time: 1 hour

Ingredients:

- 2 kgs. corned beef brisket (flat-cut)
- 340 grams sliced celery
- 2 small unpeeled and sliced oranges
- 2 small thinly sliced onions
- 2 chopped garlic cloves
- 3 halved bay leaves
- 1 tbsp. dill
- 4 halved cinnamon sticks
- 500 ml water

Instructions:

1. Soak the beef brisket in water for about an hour. Drain immediately before cooking.
2. Place the beef brisket in the pressure cooker. If the meat is too big, divide it in half. Add all the other ingredients. Put just enough water to cover the meat surface.
3. Put the lid in place and lock. Put the pressure regulator properly on the vent pipe then turn on the heat to medium.
4. Allow the meat to cook for 50 minutes at 15 psi. The pressure regulator must be slowly rocking while cooking.
5. Apply the natural release method before removing the cooker from the heat and waiting for pressure to go down.
6. Carefully take the lid off, and then transfer the meat to a serving platter. Allow it to rest for about 5 minutes.
7. Slice the meat thinly, against the grain. Serve.

Chili con Carne

In just 60 minutes, you can indulge in a hot bowl of chili con carne easily prepared through pressure cooking. This is a very popular recipe the world over. A warm bowl of the dish can easily wash all your blues away. It is ideal for lunch, dinner, or as a snack on a rainy and lazy afternoon. This recipe is a healthy version. Low in sodium, but just as delectable. Serve it with rice, bread, or biscuits.

Makes 4 servings

Preparation Time: 30 minutes

Cooking Time: 30 minutes

Ingredients:

- 400 grams ground beef
- 4 tbsps. olive oil
- 1 bay leaf
- 1 chopped medium onion
- 2 finely chopped garlic cloves
- 150 grams of soaked kidney beans
- 300 grams of drained & chopped canned tomatoes
- 1 tsp tomato paste
- 1 tsp salt
- 1 tbsp chili powder
- dried basil leaves
- 1/2 tsp ground cumin
- 180 ml water

Instructions:

1. Heat one tablespoon of olive oil in the pressure cooker without the lid for 2 minutes. Allow the ground beef to cook until it turns brown before removing from the uncovered cooker.
2. Put the rest of the oil. Add the garlic and onions and stir fry until they turn light brown.
3. Toss in the beef together with the other ingredients. Stir.
4. Place the pressure cooker lid and lock. Bring the heat to high. Once the target pressure is reached, lower the heat and allow to cook for about 18 minutes.
5. Take the cooker away from the heat and allow it to cool on its own.
6. Remove the bay leaves. Serve the dish hot.

Beef Pot Roast

With this dish, dinnertime is worth looking forward to, particularly when you are coming home from a long and tiring day at the office. There is no better way to relieve your rumbling tummy and unpleasant mood than with the inviting aroma and mouth-watering taste of a perfectly done pot roast? This quick and easy to cook dish is for the whole family to enjoy.

Makes 6 to 8 servings

Preparation Time: 10 minutes

Cooking Time: 1 hour

Ingredients:

- 1.5 to 1.75 kg beef chuck roast
- 118 ml red wine
- 500 ml beef stock

- ½ tsp chicken salt
- ½ tsp smoked paprika
- ½ tsp salt
- ½ tsp black pepper
- 1 roughly chopped medium onion
- 5 chunked medium potatoes
- 4 minced garlic cloves
- 3 chunked medium carrots

Instructions:

1. Prepare the beef by trimming the excess fat off.
2. Combine the salt, paprika, black pepper and chicken salt in a small-sized bowl.
3. Thoroughly rub the salt mixture on the beef.
4. Put the beef in the pressure cooker.
5. Add the onions, garlic, red wine, and beef stock.
6. Lock the pressure cooker lid and cook for 45 to 50 minutes at high pressure.
7. Remove the cooker from the heat and apply the quick release method.
8. Check the beef for tenderness.
9. Add the carrots and potatoes; make sure to evenly distribute the veggies inside the pot.
10. Bring to pressure and allow to cook for another 5 to 10 minutes.
11. Apply the natural release method. Remove the lid and serve warm with gravy.

Pasta Casserole

You can never put a good Italian pasta dish down. The pressure cooker is used for most of the required cooking for this dish. A little help is required from your grill just for the cheese to provide the perfect crunch. This dish is perfect for the whole family to enjoy on a cold winter night.

Makes 4 servings

Preparation Time: 15 minutes

Cooking Time: 20 minutes

Ingredients:

- 500 g Rigatoni pasta
- 300 g ground beef
- 375 g shredded Mozzarella cheese
- 450 g tomato puree
- 1 celery stalk
- 1 carrot
- 1 onion
- 25 ml red wine
- salt & pepper
- butter

Instructions:

1. Pre-heat the uncovered pressure cooker at medium heat.
2. Chop the celery, onions, and carrots.
3. Add butter (around 2 tbsps.) Cook the celery, onions, and carrots for about 5 minutes or until the soften.
4. Turn up the heat to high. Put the ground beef in the cooker followed by a pinch of salt & pepper.
5. Allow to cook for about 10 minutes or until the meat turns brown on all sides.

6. After all the water has evaporated and the meat starts to sizzle, deglaze the pan by adding some wine. Cook some more to allow the wine to evaporate, which should only take about a minute.

7. Add the tomato puree and the pasta. If desired, season with salt. Pour enough water to fully cover the pasta. Then start stirring and flattening the pasta. Use as small amount of water as possible.

8. Set the cooker at low pressure and the heat at high. Upon reaching the pressure, lower the heat and allow to cook for 5 minutes more.

9. Release the pressure, and unlock the lid.

10. Stir the pot contents, allowing the pasta some time to rest.

11. Transfer half of the cooked contents to an oiled deep dish or casserole. Sprinkle some shredded cheese on top. Pour the remaining contents of the cooker on top, and sprinkle with the rest of the shredded cheese.

12. If desired, pat or brush with butter.

13. Put the casserole under the casserole for 3 minutes or just enough time to melt the cheese and achieve a golden color.

14. Serve hot and enjoy!

Additional Notes:

1. You can use biscuits or other available crumbs for the crust.

2. If you notice condensed water resting on the food after removing it from the cooker, blot it gently using a paper towel.

3. You can serve the dish topped with nutmeg, cinnamon, a dollop of whipped cream, or simply on its own.

Pork Dishes

Boneless Pork Roast w/ Fennel

No meat-lover can resist this flavorful and succulent dish. This succulent and aromatic dish, with the meticulous preparation it demands, is a big hit for lunch or dinner. The best part is that you can prepare this dish in only two hours with the help of a pressure cooker – this is a lot quicker than whipping up the dish using traditional cooking methods.

Makes 4 servings

Preparation Time: 20 minutes

Cooking Time: 1 hour 20 minutes

Ingredients:

- 2 tbsps. olive oil
- 1 kilo boneless pork
- salt & ground pepper, to taste
- 1 sliced onion
- 2 cloves of peeled & crushed garlic
- 150 ml chicken stock
- 150 ml white wine
- ½ kg thickly sliced fennel bulbs

Instructions:

1. Put olive oil in the pressure cooker (heavy based) at high heat.

2. Add the pork seasoned w/ a pinch of salt & pepper; cook until a brown color is achieved on all sides.
3. Transfer the roast from the heat into a plate. Set it aside for a while.
4. Put the garlic into the cooker, followed by the chicken stock and white wine. Bring it to a boil. Using a wooden spoon, scrape the bottom to retrieve the juices.
5. Put the roast back into the pressure cooker. Cover it and let it cook for 35 to 40 minutes.
6. Carefully remove the pressure cooker lid to add the fennel and sliced onion.
7. Place the lid again and cook for another 15 minutes or just until the veggies tenderize.
8. Get the cooker out of the heat. Remove the roast and vegetables. Keep everything warm using a separate dish.
9. Put the pressure cooker back at medium heat, uncovered. Wait a few minutes to let the sauce cook. If you prefer sticky and thicker sauce, add a tsp. of flour, then stir constantly.
10. Serve the roast along with the sauce and fennel mix.

Pork Loin w/ Veggies

Perfectly roasted pork loin paired with fresh and crisp veggies – heavenly! This pressure cooker recipe introduces an exciting and savory new way to enjoy the popular dish. With its enhanced flavor, there is no wonder you will come back for a second serving.

Makes 4 servings

Preparation Time: 15 minutes

Cooking Time: 45 minutes

Ingredients:

- 900 grams boneless top roast pork loin
- 250 ml water
- 3 sliced carrots
- 6 garlic cloves
- 3 quartered potatoes
- 1 quartered onion
- salt & pepper
- 2 sliced celery stalks
- 1 bay leaf
- 2 tbsps. of vegetable oil

Instructions:

1. Using a paring knife, slit the pork loin on top, about 2 to 3 cm. deep.
2. Cut a hole in between the slits, big enough to insert the garlic cloves. Push the cloves entirely into the meat.
3 To taste, season with salt & pepper.
4. Put the vegetable oil and cook the pork at medium high heat. Allow to cook until all the sides are browned.
5. Drain the excess oil after cooking.
6. Put the water in the pot. (Do this only after the cooker cools down.)
7. Put the bay leaf.
8. Put the pork on the trivet or cooking rack.
9. Put the lid w/ the pressure regulator securely on the vent pipe.
10 Allow to cook at 15 psi for half an hour.
11. After 30 minutes, cool the cooker immediately and take the meat out.
12. Put the veggies on the trivet or rack.
13. Put the meat back on top of the veggies.
14. Securely close the lid with the regulator on the vent.

15. Allow to cook at 15 psi for 5 minutes more.
16. Immediately allow the cooker to cool down then take the meat and veggies out.
17. Allow the meat to rest for about 5 minutes. Carve and serve.

Additional Notes:

1. To fully maximize the flavor of the veggies, chop them into 2 to 3 cm pieces.
2. You can adjust the number of garlic holes to achieve the level of garlic flavor you prefer.
3. Make sure that each time you put the pressure cooker lid, the contents do not exceed 2/3 of the cooker's full capacity.
4. After the dish is done, use the remaining liquids in the cooker as sauce.

Char Siu (Chinese-Style Pork Barbecue)

Everyone loves barbecue parties. This dish is perfect for a weekend BBQ party with family and friends. But instead of the good old-fashioned grill, the dish is cooked with a pressure cooker. Best served green veggies, rice, and barbecue sauce, this is great barbecue with a twist.

Makes 6 servings

Preparation Time: 15 minutes

Cooking Time: 50 minutes

Ingredients:

- 1 kg trimmed pork belly

- 4 tbsps soy sauce
- 1 liter chicken stock
- 8 tbsps. of char siu sauce (you can get it in Asian food/deli stores)
- 2 tbsps honey
- 1 tsp peanut oil
- 2 tbsps dry sherry
- 2 tsps sesame oil

Instructions:

1. Mix the soy sauce, stock, sherry, and ½ of the prepared char siu sauce at medium heat in the pressure cooker with lid off.
2. Allow to cook for 5 to 8 minutes.
3. Put the pork belly in. Place the lid on and bring to the target pressure. Reduce the heat to medium for half an hour more.
4. Let the cooker cool down naturally.
5. Take the pork out and let it cool down. Do not throw away the remaining cooking liquid.
6. Chop the cooked pork belly into even-sized pieces.
7. Heat the peanut oil in a frying pan at medium high heat. Let the pork cook.
8. Mix the sesame oil, honey, and the remaining char siu sauce in a separate bowl.
9. Use the mix to brush the pork belly pieces while cooking for ten minutes or until it is fully coated and brown.
10. Pour the leftover cooking liquid in a saucepan and cook it at medium high heat.
11. Allow it to boil before reducing the heat. Simmer for about 3 minutes.
12. Pour the mixture over the pork. Serve and enjoy.

Lamb Dishes

Lamb Shanks

Tender and with meat falling off the bone, perfectly cooked lamb shanks ready to eat in only half an hour. This dish is the perfect dinner for the whole family after a long day at work or school. Pressure cooking makes this dish even more tender and savory.

Makes 4 servings

Preparation Time: 15 minutes

Cooking Time: 45 minutes

Ingredients:

- 4 lamb shanks
- 2 tbsps olive oil
- 60 g plain flour
- 1 chopped large onion
- 3 large carrots, chopped into medium-sized pieces
- 1 tsp oregano
- 2 tbsps of tomato paste
- 2 crushed garlic cloves
- 1 quartered medium tomato
- 1 beef bouillon cube
- 60 ml water
- 180 ml red wine
- salt & pepper

Instructions:

1. Put all the flour in a shallow container then add a dash of salt & pepper. Mix.
2. Roll the shanks in the mixture to coat.
3. Put olive oil in the cooker and heat at medium to high setting.
4. Allow the lamb shanks to brown in the hot oil before transferring to a plate.
5. Use the same oil to sauté the crushed garlic, chopped onion, carrots, and oregano for 4 to 5 minutes or until the slices of onion are translucent.
6. Place the quartered tomato, tomato paste, water, bouillon cube, and red wine.
7. Stir and allow to boil before putting back the lamb shanks in.
8. Place the lid and lock. Bring until the desired pressure is achieved.
9. Reduce the heat to low and continue cooking for another 20 to 25 minutes.
10 Use the natural method to release the pressure.
11. Take the lamb shanks out of the cooker and transfer to a serving dish.
12. Serve and enjoy!

Additional Notes:

If you want your gravy thicker, mix 1 ½ tbsps. of water with 2 tbsps. of plain starch to create a paste. Once the lamb is removed from the cooker, stir the paste into the leftover sauce. Serving the dish with some fluffy mashed potatoes is highly recommended.

Lamb Barley Stew

Comfort food comes in various forms, depending on personal preference – fried chicken, soups, desserts, steak, and many others. If you want to try something new, but hearty and delicious, nonetheless, try this pressure cooked stew dish that is sure to satisfy your cravings and fill your tummy!

Makes 4 servings

Preparation Time: 20 minutes

Cooking Time: 45 minutes

Ingredients:

- 1 cooked leg of lamb, cooked
- 200 g barley
- 5 carrots
- 150 g frozen peas
- 3 onions
- 500 ml water
- 250 ml beef broth

Instructions:

1. Separate the lamb meat from the leg bone. Cut into bite-size pieces.
2. Put the bone in the cooker.
3. Put some water, broth, and barley into the pressure cooker.
4. Cook with the lid on at high heat.
5. Upon reaching the desired high pressure, reduce the heat just enough to maintain the pressure. Allow to cook for 20 minutes more.
6. Release the pressure once the cook time is over.
7. Remove the lid. Take the bone out of the cooker. Put back the residual meat that stuck to the bone back into the cooker.
8. Put the quartered onions and sliced carrots into the pressure cooker.
9. Cook for 10 minutes more at high heat.

10. Release the pressure once cooked.
11. Add the meat and peas.
12. Serve and enjoy!

Additional Notes:

1. Leftover lamb meat is great for this recipe. Any type of red meat like beef or pork can also be used.
2. If preferred, you can add more vegetables to the dish like green beans and tomatoes.
3. If beef broth is not available, you can replace it with 2 bouillon cubes. Just make sure to add 250 ml of water.
4. You can adjust the water to beef broth ratio, depending on your preference.

Chapter 5: Pressure Cooker Recipes – Fish and Seafood Dishes

Fish Chowder

On their own, chowders are hearty, delicious and filling meals. However, they also make great starters or sides. Here is a tasty fish chowder recipe, made easier to prepare using your pressure cooker.

Makes 4 to 6 servings

Preparation Time: 15 minutes

Cooking Time: 25 minutes

Ingredients:

- 500 g skinless and boneless haddock or another type white fish, sliced into medium chunks
- 350 g washed and peeled potatoes, chopped into medium-sized chunks
- 350 ml milk
- 450 ml water
- 1 finely chopped small onion,
- 470 ml chicken stock
- 470 ml half & half (4 parts of whole milk w/ 1 part heavy cream)
- Salt & pepper, to taste

Instructions:

1. Put the fish chunks, chicken stock, milk, and water into the pressure cooker.
2. Cover the cooker and lock the lid; bring to pressure at medium-high heat. Allow to cook for another 8 to 10 minutes once pressure is reached.
3. Take the cooker away from the heat and naturally release the pressure.
4. Carefully open the cooker and without the pressure cooker lid, bring the heat to medium low.
5. Add some salt & pepper to taste.
6. Stir the half & half in and stir continuously until the chowder has thickened slightly.
7. Remove the cooker from the heat. Garnish the dish as desired.
8. Serve and enjoy!

Mediterranean Style Fish

You will find this dish unique if you have been accustomed to pairing steamed fish with lemon. This recipe calls for a combination of capers and tomatoes for a tasty, but at the same time sweet, and somewhat vinegary end result.

Makes 4 servings

Preparation Time: 5 minutes

Cooking Time: 10 minutes

Ingredients:

- 4 fillets of white fish
- 500g halved cherry tomatoes
- 1 pressed clove of garlic

- 2 tbsps. of pickled capers
- 1 cup of Taggiesche olives
- thyme
- olive oil
- salt & pepper (optional)

Instructions:

1. Put the cherry tomato halves at pit of a heat-proof bowl.
2. Put in some fresh thyme.
3. Top the tomatoes with the fish.
4. Add the olive oil, crushed garlic, and a pinch of salt.
5. Put everything including the bowl inside the cooker.
6. Turn up the heat to high, and set the pressure cooker to low. After reaching pressure, lower the heat and allow to cook for 5 more minutes.
7. Once the cooking time is over, release the pressure using the natural method.
8. Serve individually in separate plates. Garnish with more herbs and cherry tomatoes on top. Enjoy!

Octopus and Potatoes

Tough and rubbery consistency – this is probably the first thing that comes to your mind upon hearing about an octopus dish, right? Add the fact that it is difficult to prepare and cook, and not to mention eat! However, there is a secret to properly tenderizing the flesh prior to cooking. Not too many people are aware of that, and this recipe will let you in on that big secret!

Makes 6 servings

Preparation Time: 20 minutes

Cooking Time: 35 minutes

Ingredients:

- 1 kg octopus
- 3 garlic cloves
- 1 kg potatoes
- chopped parsley
- 1 bay leaf
- 125 ml olive oil
- 1/2 tsp peppercorns
- 5 tbsps vinegar
- salt & pepper

Instructions:

1. To clean the octopus properly, remove the head, halve the body and then turn it inside out. Remove everything inside, including the eyes. Find the area where the tentacles meet and take out the beak. Put under running water to rinse. Then set it aside.
2. Thoroughly wash the potatoes and put them in the pressure cooker unpeeled. Add just enough water to cover half of the potatoes then season w/ salt.
3. Place the lid and lock. Set the heat to high. When the pan starts to whistle, lower the burner to medium low. Allow to cook for 15 minutes at this temperature.
4. Release the vapor afterwards. Using tongs, take the potatoes out. Do not discard the remaining cooking water.
5. Using a fork and tongs, peel the potatoes. Put some water just enough to almost cover the octopus entirely.

6. Add the bay leaf, pepper, a pinch of salt and a clove of garlic. Bring to a boil.
7. Put the octopus in the pressure cooker, tentacles first.
8. Put the lid and lock. Allow to cook at high heat until pressure is reached. Afterwards, lower the heat to minimum temperature, just enough to maintain the pressure. Let it cook for another 20 minutes.
9. When done coking, release pressure then open the cooker carefully. By this time, the octopus flesh should have enough tenderness to allow a fork to easily sink through. If not, cook for 2 or 3 minutes more.
10. Strain off the liquids. Chop the octopus flesh into bite-size pieces and set aside.
11. Mix the vinegar, olive oil, salt & pepper, and crushed garlic cloves in a small container or jar then seal. Thoroughly shake to blend all the flavors together. This mixture will be your vinaigrette.
12. By now, the potatoes should have cooled down. Chop them into chunks the same size of the octopus.
13. Mix all the ingredients in a bowl. Put chili, chopped parsley on top. Tightly cover the bowl then refrigerate before serving.

Additional Notes:

1. If desired, remove the skin of the octopus using the backside of a knife before serving.
2. You can use other spices and herbs you want to season and garnish the cooked dish.
3. If you don't have enough time to cook, you can cook the octopus and the potatoes at the same time, but this will make the potatoes purplish in color because of the skin of the octopus seeping into the cooking liquid.
4. For best results, tenderize the octopus before cooking, particularly if bought fresh. This can be done by storing it in the freezer for one whole day before defrosting.

Salmon Al Cartoccio

In Italian, al cartoccio directly translates to packet cooking. It is called en pallion in France. Basically, it is a way to cook fish by steaming in its own zest and juices, with some veggies on the side. This is a good way to cook fish, but since it is very delicate, it must be protected from the turbulence of the pressure cooker. Thus, the fish is thoroughly wrapped in oven paper or foil or both.

Makes 4 servings

Preparation Time: 20 minutes

Cooking Time: 15 minutes

Ingredients:

- 4 fresh or frozen salmon fillets
- 3 sliced tomatoes
- 1 shaved white onion
- 1 sliced lemon
- 4 sprigs of thyme
- 4 sprigs of parsley
- olive oil
- salt & pepper, to taste

Instructions:

1. Arrange all the ingredients on parchment paper using this order – swirl of oil, 1 potato layer, salt & pepper and oil, fish

fillet, salt & pepper and oil, herbs and onion rings, slices of lemon, salt, and oil.
2. Next, fold the packet and wrap it in tinfoil snugly.
3. Pour 2 cups of water into the pressure cooker. Put the steamer basket in proper position then lay the packet on top.
4. Cook 2 fillets at a time. If your cooker is tall or large enough, you can use 2 layers of baskets simultaneously.
5. Seal the pressure cooker with its lead. Set to high heat and wait until target pressure is reached. Turn the heat down to minimum setting.
6. The cooking time should be in the vicinity of 12 to 15 minutes. You can release the vapor afterwards, but don't open the top just yet.
7. Allow the fish packets to sit inside the locked cooker for about 5 minutes more.
8. Carefully open the cooker and take the packets out. Remove the tinfoil. Serve and enjoy!

Additional Notes:

1. This fish recipe is ideal for any drained and thawed white fish fillet such as grouper.
2. You can replace lemons with white wine.
3. If you want, you can experiment with various spices and herbs.
4. Make sure there is enough spacing between packets when cooking.
5. To achieve the desired thin slices of onions and potatoes, use a mandolin slicer.

Coconut Fish Curry

Curry dishes are distinctly Indian cuisine, even with all the different versions in terms of cooking style and ingredients. The pair of fish and coconut is probably the top favorite in the world to cook with earthly spices and herbs. This is best illustrated with this pressure cooker recipe version of the rich and spicy classic Indian dish that is prefect for dinner or lunch.

Makes 6 to 8 servings

Preparation Time: 5 minutes

Cooking Time: 15 minutes

Ingredients:

- 750 g fish fillets, rinsed and cut in bite-size pieces
- 500 ml coconut milk (unsweetened)
- 1 chopped tomato
- 2 capsicums, sliced into strips
- 2 squeezed garlic cloves
- 6 curry leaves
- 2 onions, sliced into strips
- 2 tsps of ground cumin
- 1 tbsp of ground coriander
- 1/2 tsp of ground turmeric
- 1 tbsp of freshly grated ginger
- 1 tsp of hot pepper flakes
- 1/2 tsp of ground fenugreek
- lemon juice
- salt

Instructions:

1. Pre-hat the cooker at medium low without cover.
2. Put the oil and the curry leaves then fry for one minute.
3. Add the garlic, ginger, and onion. Sauté until tender.

4. Put the 5 ground spices (cumin, coriander, fenugreek, hot pepper, and turmeric.) Together with the onions, sauté for 2 minutes.
5. To deglaze, add the coconut milk. Make sure that nothing remains stuck to the cooker's bottom.
6. Add the fish, tomatoes, and capsicum. Stir to make sure that the fish is coated with the mixture very well.
7. Set the level of heat to high, and the pressure level to low. Upon reaching pressure, turn down the heat to low.
8. Cook at low pressure for 5 minutes.
9. Release the vapor to release the pressure.
10. To taste, season with salt then spritz the dish on top with lemon juice.

Additional Notes:

1. If unavailable, you can substitute fresh fish with frozen or thawed fish.
2. A good alternative to tomatoes is 1 cup of cherry tomatoes.
3. If fresh ginger is not available, you can replace it with 1/8 tsp. of ginger powder.
4. For curry leaves, good alternatives are basil, bay leaves or kaffir lime leaves.
5. In lieu of hot pepper flakes, you can opt to use chili powder.
6. For the 5 spices, you can use 3 tablespoons of curry powder mix.

Chapter 6: Pressure Cooker Recipes – Vegetarian Dishes

Pumpkin Soup

Halloween is the time of year when people have a great time making horrifying or fun jack-o-lantern faces but once the occasion is over, what remains are chunks of pumpkins that need to be consumed. So, what can you do other than the usual pie? That's it: pumpkin soup. Here is an easy to prepare dish using your pressure cooker. Add bay leaves and grated apple into the mix and what do you get? Pumpkin soup that is delicious in its own subtle way!

Makes 12 servings

Preparation Time: 25 minutes

Cooking Time: 25 minutes

Ingredients:

- 1 tbsp butter
- Butternut pumpkin chunks
- 1 diced potato
- 1 peeled, cored and grated apple
- 1 chopped brown onion
- 4 bay leaves
- 750 ml of chicken stock
- Cracked black pepper
- Curry powder
- 500 ml milk

Instructions:

1. Melt the butter in the cooker.
2. Add the chunks of pumpkin, onion, potato, and a bit of curry powder. Cook at low heat gently until the onion slightly turns brown while occasionally stirring.
3. Next, add the chicken stock, bay leaves, and black pepper.
4. Seal the pressure cooker before bringing to pressure. Allow to cook for about 5 minutes.
5. Use the cold water method to release pressure.
6. Stir the grated apple in, and cook for 10 minutes without the pressure cooker cover. Stir occasionally.
7. Take the bay leaves out. Transfer the remaining contents of the cooker into a blender. Process. Add some milk until the soup is smooth and creamy.
8. Serve warm in bowls. The soup is best served with croutons.

Vegetarian Chili

Chili is easily one of the Mexican foods popular the world over. With its spicy, delectable goodness, it warms the heart and fills the tummy. This dish will keep you going on a cold day. With this pressure cooker recipe, you will get not only the full chili flavor without the meat, but you get to enjoy this Mexican dish in less than 30 minutes. That's amazing considering that beans take a lifetime to soften using traditional cooking methods.

Makes 6 to 8 servings

Preparation Time: 15 minutes

Cooking Time: 30 minutes

Ingredients:

- 225 grams pinto beans (soaked overnight prior to cooking)
- 225 grams red kidney beans (soaked overnight prior to cooking)
- 375 grams roughly chopped Roma tomatoes
- 900 ml water
- 2 roughly chopped onions
- 1 pack ground round Yves veggie
- 3 minced garlic cloves, minced
- 1 diced capsicum, diced
- 2 tsps cumin
- 1 bay leaf
- 2 tbsps of olive oil
- 1 ½ tsps oregano
- 1 tbsp chilli powder(put more if spicier chili is preferred)
- Salt, to taste

Instructions:

1. At medium setting, heat olive oil in the cooker.
2. Sauté the garlic cloves and onions until translucent.
3. Add the ground round veggie and cook until brown. Then toss in the cumin, capsicum, oregano, chili powder, salt, and bay leaf. Mix everything well.
4. Add the beans, water, and tomatoes. Stir.
5. Cover the pressure cooker and lock. Bring to pressure and allow to cook for about 20 minutes.
6. Take the cooker away from the heat and release pressure using the natural method.
7. Take the bay leaf out. Serve the dish while still hot, with grated cheddar cheese or sour cream for toppings; best enjoyed with homemade cornbread.

Lemoned Broccoli

One of the most popular vegetables, broccoli is often used as a side dish, and as ingredient in soups, salads, and different appetizers. Some people, however, prefer to keep things simple. Steamed broccoli on its own is a tasty and interesting side dish, but when eaten too often, it gets a bit boring. With this recipe, you will discover how adding an ingredient or two can make a huge difference!

Makes 4 to 6 servings

Preparation Time: 5 minutes

Cooking Time: 2 minutes

Ingredients:

- 900 grams of broccoli
- 125 ml water
- 4 slices of lemon
- salt & pepper, to taste

Instructions:

1. Remove the broccoli stalks' tough parts.
2. Score the ends.
3. Put some water in the cooker.
4. Put the broccoli sprinkled w/ lemon juice.
5. As desired, season w/ salt & pepper.
6. Close and seal the pressure cooker.
7. Allow to cook for no more than 2 minutes at 15 psi.

8. Allow to cool down after cooking.
9. Serve on its own or with a main dish.

Additional Notes:

1. The dish is best served with meats and rice.
2. If desired, you can add some cooked red onions to the dish.
3. Only use fresh broccoli for this recipe.

Risotto with Artichoke Hearts

Risotto is traditionally an Italian rice dish, and is among the most frequently used method to prepare and eat rice in the country. This is just another one of the many versions.

Makes 4 servings

Preparation Time: 15 minutes

Cooking Time: 15 minutes

Ingredients:

- 175 g of chocolate graham cracker crumbs
- 2 x 240 g packages of cream cheese, softened
- 180 g Arborio rice
- 400 g artichoke hearts, chopped
- 25 g Parmesan cheese
- 250 ml chicken stock
- 250 ml water
- 40 ml white wine
- 2 garlic cloves, minced

- 1 1/2 tbsp fresh thyme
- 1 tbsp olive oil
- salt and pepper

Instructions:

1. At medium setting, heat the oil in the cooker.
2. Cook the rice for 2 minutes.
3. Put in the garlic and allow to cook for about a minute.
4. Get a bowl that fits properly in the pressure cooker. Mix the stock, wine, and garlic with the rice in the bowl. Cover the bowl with tinfoil.
5. Put some water in the pressure cooker.
6. Place the bowl on a steaming basket or cooking rack, and then put it inside the cooker.
7. Properly close and lock the pressure cooker lid, making sure that the regulator is placed properly o the vent pipe.
8. Allow to cook at 15 psi for about 8 minutes.
9. Once cooked, let the pressure naturally drop down.
10. Take the bowl out of the pressure cooker. Remove the tinfoil.
11. Put the cheese artichoke hearts, and thyme I the cooked dish.
12. Serve hot and enjoy!

Additional Notes:

1. Instead of fresh thyme, you can opt to use dry thyme, if desired.
2. Make a foil lifter if the bowl doesn't have handles or is difficult to remove from the cooker.
3. You can add other veggies you want in the risotto.

Vegetable Curry

You've probably done a variety of curry recipes before, but usually with meats like lamb, beef, and chicken, among others. This recipe will allow you to try a healthier version of the popular Indian dish – using various veggies.

Makes 6 servings

Preparation Time: 20 minutes

Cooking Time: 10 minutes

Ingredients:

- 3 potatoes
- 2 sweet potatoes
- 1 red onion
- 2 capsicums
- 275 g green peas
- 400 g of rinsed chickpeas
- 25 g chopped coriander
- 70 g chopped toasted almonds
- 90 ml of non-sweetened coconut milk
- 6 tbsps of mild curry paste
- 65 ml water

Instructions:

1. Heat some oil in the pressure cooker.
2. Put the onions in, and then sauté with salt & pepper for about 5 minutes.
3. Add the sweet potatoes, potatoes, curry paste, capsicum, water, and coconut milk.

4. Cover and lock the pressure cooker and allow it to reach the desired pressure.
5. Lower the heat to maintain the pressure. Allow to cook for 2 more minutes or until the veggies are all tender.
6. Release pressure using the quick release method. This is done by putting the cooker under running water with the lid on.
7. Once the pressure is released, carefully open the lead and then add the chickpeas and peas.
8. Garnish the dish with toasted almonds and coriander.
9. Serve and enjoy!

Additional Notes:

1. Vegetable is great with basmati rice.
2. If you prefer some meat in your curry, just sauté some skinless chicken thighs cut in chunks, and mix with the veggies.
3. You can adjust the spiciness of the dish by using a milder or hotter variety of curry paste.

Conclusion

I'd like to thank you and congratulate you for transiting my lines from start to finish.

I hope this book was able to help you to learn the basics of pressure cooking, as well as important tips on how to maximize the use of your pressure cooker. Now it's time to apply everything that you learned from this book and start whipping healthy and tasty pressure cooked meals that the whole family will enjoy.

It's time for you to transcend the written word and keep on fighting for what you want in life. Go out there and fight for what is yours!

I wish you the best of luck!

Part 2

Introduction

The *"Pressure Cooker Cookbook"* contains detailed, but easy to follow recipes that you can use for your daily meals. Many people believe that pressure cookers are complicated pieces of machinery. Truth is with a little foresight and planning, this kitchen equipment can help you make fast and delicious meals, without spending all day in the kitchen.

With this book, you will learn the basics of electric pressure cooking. There are also cooking tips on how to make your dishes flavorful and healthier at the same time. These recipes cater to a whole range of diet preferences (e.g. vegetarian, lactose-intolerant, gluten-free, etc.) and may be served to adults and children alike.

I hope you learn a lot from this book, and become comfortable using electric pressure cookers all the time.

Thanks again for downloading this book. I hope you enjoy it!

Chapter 1: Creating Clean And Healthy Meals With The Electric Pressure Cooker

Did you know that even professional chefs feel intimidated about using pressure cookers? Many would opt for deep fryers, slow cookers, smokers, or ovens instead. This may stem from the fact that earlier models were cumbersome, and even dangerous to cook with on a regular basis.

Fortunately, pressure cookers have been improved a thousand-fold since.

Most electric pressure cookers are multi-purpose. Some can be used as rice cookers, slow cookers, steamers, sterilizers, and yogurt makers. One of the best and newest features is the sauté option (sometimes called boil function,) where you can cook your flavor base or brown the meat right in the same pot. This gives you one less pan to wash every time you cook.

Fully automated electric pressure cookers allow you to create tasty and healthy dishes without having to stay in the kitchen all day.

Here are a couple of questions people often ask about electric pressure cookers.

Question: *Is it true that stovetop pressure cookers cook faster than the electric pressure cooker?*

Answer: Yes, you can turn up the heat higher on a stovetop, whereas an electric pressure cooker has limited heat settings.

However, a stovetop pressure cooker's internal and external temperatures must be constantly monitored and carefully maintained. Otherwise, you either undercook or overcook the food, and you risk destroying the cooker itself by subjecting it to too much pressure.

Quickly releasing pressure after cooking can also be a hazardous affair. You always have to bring the stovetop cooker to the sink when doing so, or you will never get the lid off. Worse still, if you are not careful enough, the steam from the natural and quick pressure release can cause 3rd degree burns.

Older models of pressure cookers have been known to literally explode under too much pressure.

Modern day electric pressure cookers can be programmed to reach the desired internal temperature and the amount of pressure needed for cooking. These have built-in timers and automatic pressure release systems that allow you to cook safely without being physically near the machine.

Question: *Why should I buy an electric pressure cooker when a stovetop pressure cooker is much cheaper?*

Here is a fair comparison between electric and stovetop pressure cookers.

Feature #1 : Price
Electric Pressure Cooker : About 25% to 200% more expensive than its stovetop counterpart. Prices would still depend on availability, size, capacity, and brand.
Stovetop Pressure Cooker : Some good quality models are very affordable.
Conclusion : Stovetop Pressure Cooker Wins!

Feature #2 : Cooking Time
Electric Pressure Cooker : Because the heat setting is fully automated and can only go as high as deemed safe by the manufacturers, it takes about 4 to 6 minutes longer for the pressure to build up within the cooking pot. This prolongs cooking time by 1% to 10% as compared to its stovetop counterpart.
Stovetop Pressure Cooker : The heat can be turned as high as the stovetop (or any heat source, e.g. open flame) can manage. This helps build up the pressure quickly, and makes cooking dishes faster too.
Conclusion : Stovetop Pressure Cooker Wins!

Feature #3 : Portability
Electric Pressure Cooker : This cooker needs a flat, level, and dry surface to stand on, and an uninterrupted supply of electricity (when cooking.)
Stovetop Pressure Cooker : As long as there is a heat source hot enough, this type of cooker can be used just about anywhere. You can even use this over open flame like campfires and barbecue pits.
Conclusion : Stovetop Pressure Cooker Wins!

Feature #4 : Maximum Pressure Buildup and Pressure Settings

Electric Pressure Cooker : The most efficient electric pressure cookers can only provide 13 psi (pounds per square inch) of pressure. Others only provide 11, 10, 9, 8 or 6 psi. Cooking time needs to be adjusted depending on how efficient your cooker is. Settings can be confusing because some electric cookers have dizzying arrays of pressure controls (e.g. high, medium high, medium, medium low, low, meat setting, fish setting, rice setting, etc.) This is especially true for multi-purpose pressure cookers. Some of the most common settings may include sauté, slow cook, simmer, roast, rice, stew, soup, steam, etc.

Stovetop Pressure Cooker : Most stovetop cookers can reach 15 psi. This makes cooking faster, and following standard recipes easier. Settings are also clear-cut.

Cooking settings are limited to:

* Low (cooking) pressure

* High (cooking) pressure

Pressure release settings are limited to:

* Quick release - cold/tap running water should be poured over the lid. This brings down the core temperature quickly.

* Normal release - (sometimes called slow release) slower form of pressure release that happens *after cooking*. There is no need to subject the stovetop pressure cooker to water.

* Natural release - or also known as leaky lid release. Newer models of stovetop pressure cookers now have this option. This releases steam on its own *during cooking*, especially when the internal pressure builds up far too quickly, at a short amount of time. This prevents the cookers from literally exploding on the stove.

Conclusion : Stovetop Pressure Cooker Wins!

Cooking Tip #1: When cooking with meats, always make sure you either use properly defrosted meat or better still, fresh cuts from the market. If you try to cook frozen meat in an electric pressure cooker, its internal temperature would take a long time to reach boiling point. Either extend its cooking time, or you risk undercooking the meat. This would also shorten the durability of your pressure cooker's internal heater, and void manufacturer's warranty.

Feature #5 : Pressure Release Time

Electric Pressure Cooker : Being fully automated, and with its thermos-like insulation, the quick pressure release time of the electric cooker is delayed by as much as 15 minutes, as compared to its stovetop counterpart. The normal or slow pressure release takes 15 to 25 minutes longer.

Stovetop Pressure Cooker : Pressure release is quickly facilitated by running the cooker under cold/tap running water. This could take as little as 2 minutes. Normal pressure release would only take 5 to 10 minutes longer.

Conclusion : Stovetop Pressure Cooker Wins!

Feature #6 : Heat Dissipation

Electric Pressure Cooker : Heat is contained within the thermos-like walls of the pressure cooker. This makes cooking 55% to 75% more efficient than its stovetop counterpart. Because heat is contained and unlikely to transfer anywhere, you can leave a (properly programmed) pressure cooker in the kitchen unattended when cooking.

Stovetop Pressure Cooker : Like all stovetop cookeries, heat dissipates from the source to the surrounding air. This makes it difficult to maintain constant pressure within the pot. You have to constantly adjust the heat or flame. You also have to check the indicator on the lid to see if the right amount of pressure is building up. If the pressure is too low, the dish would take a longer time to cook. If the pressure is too high, the dish might burn. Worst case scenario: the cooker will explode, sending hot food and liquid everywhere.

It is also inadvisable to leave your stovetop cooker unattended for whatever reason, to prevent fire from accidentally spreading out.

Conclusion : Electric Pressure Cooker Wins!

Cooking Tip #2: Always opt for low pressure and a shorter cooking time when you prepare (almost dry or with very little cooking liquid) seafood dishes in the electric pressure cooker. The last thing you want is overcooked fish (which can flake away in the pot,) shrimp (turns rubbery,) or shellfish (shrivels away to almost nothing. You should cook seafood dishes at low pressure for 2 to 3 minutes only. Thicker cuts of fish steaks (but not those of tuna, blue marlin or salmon) can be cooked for up to 10 minutes with little moisture, but no more. Fish or other seafood items cooked with more than 3 cups of liquid are exceptions to this rule.

Feature #7 : Heat / Pressure Regulation

Electric Pressure Cooker : The electric pressure cooker has heat settings, as well as settings for type of pressure, timer and pressure release. You can simply program the desired cooking temperature, internal pressure, cooking duration and type of release, then walk away.

Stovetop Pressure Cooker : You need to manually adjust the heat before and after clamping on the cooker's lid. After that, you still need to watch the pot carefully for signs of burning. Because external temperature affects the internal pressure, you need to constantly adjust the heat under the cooker. A sudden drop or rise in room temperature can throw off the internal pressure in a hurry.

Keeping watch on the time is also crucial. It is very easy to overcook food on stovetop cookers.

Lastly, you have to be careful when releasing the pressure to avoid unwanted burns. Even experienced chefs make the mistake of releasing pressure too quickly. This can result to

sudden bursts of pressurized steam that can leave nasty burns on the hands, arms and face.
Worst case scenario: the stovetop pressure cooker explodes.
Conclusion : Electric Pressure Cooker Wins!

Feature #8 : Safety
Electric Pressure Cooker : Full automation of the product allows you to cook away from the kitchen. You can chuck in the ingredients of the desired dish into the cooker, program its cooking time/pressure/duration, and walk away. When it's done cooking, the electric cooker will release pressure on its own, which minimizes the risk of burns.
The exterior of most electric pressure cookers these days are made from thermal-coated plastic. It is relatively safe to touch even when the machine is on. This feature is also helpful in keeping your food warm hours after you have finished cooking. This allows you to preprogram your meals hours beforehand, then come back to still warm dishes.
Stovetop Pressure Cooker : When cooking anything on the stovetop, there is always a high risk of burns from direct contact with active heat sources (including open flames from old stovetop models, campfires, or barbecue pits.) If you are not careful, the hot cooking surface and steam from the released pressure can burn your hands, arms, and face.
Conclusion : Electric Pressure Cooker Wins!

Feature #9 : Multiple Functions
Electric Pressure Cooker : Many newer models have multiple functions like slow cooking, steaming, sterilizing/canning and even yogurt making. Pricier models may include sautéing functions. A few can even be converted into deep fryers.
Stovetop Pressure Cooker : You can use the base of the stovetop pressure cooker as a normal cooking pot or pan.
Conclusion : Electric Pressure Cooker Wins!

Feature #10 : Ease of Cleaning

Electric Pressure Cooker : Most models these days have non-stick, scratch free interiors that make cleaning after cooking a breeze. The actual cooking pot and lid (which is different from the exterior container and lid) can fit in most dishwashers. The exterior container and lid are usually made from thermal-resistant plastic that is easy to wipe down. The plastic is also treated to be mold and smell resistant.

Stovetop Pressure Cooker : Many stovetop pressure cookers have no or very little non-stick coating which makes cleaning somewhat tedious. Only the base of the cooking pot can be placed in the dishwasher. The lid must be carefully washed and dried by hand to prevent the electronics embedded in it from shorting out due to moisture buildup.

Unfortunately, poor maintenance on the lid can cause potentially dangerous mold buildup. This is one of the many reasons why lids are usually the first to be damaged.

Conclusion : Electric Pressure Cooker Wins!

Cooking Tip #3: Never overload your pressure cooker with food. Packing ingredients into the pot, or filling it to the brim with ingredients (and/or liquid) can affect its cooking time drastically. It would take a long time before the right amount of pressure builds up, which can leave your dish undercooked or raw. Fill your pressure cooker's pot only halfway or 2/3 full. Go easy on the liquids too. If you need to cook a large volume of food, try cooking these in separate batches.

Feature #11 : Durability

Electric Pressure Cooker : Because this equipment sits on the countertop most of the time and has a separate interior cooking lid and pot, it has less risk of electronic damage. Heat transfers are also less likely to happen due to its plastic thermal coating. At most, newer models have 3-year warranties.

Stovetop Pressure Cooker : Some manufacturers offer 20-year warranties on their product. However, if you look at the fine print, these only extend to the actual cooking pot/pan. The warranties do not include the lid, or handle, or clamp (locking mechanism.)

Often, the electronics on the lid are the first to go. This might be due to poor handling, improper storage, or improper cleaning.

The handles go next. Damage of this kind often stems from the constant moving of the pot from the stove, to the kitchen counter, to the dishwasher, and into the storage. Placing a large volume of food into the cooker and lifting it by the handle alone can contribute to its breakage as well.

The clamps go next. This often happens when the cooker is filled with too much food, or when the pressure becomes too great that it cannot be contained anymore.

Conclusion : Electric Pressure Cooker Wins!

Feature #12 : Ease of Use

Electric Pressure Cooker : With a few press of the button, you can leave your machine in the kitchen unattended while you do something else. When you come back, you simply have open the lid and ladle out the cooked meal. Afterwards, you remove the interior pot and lid, give these a rinse and place these in the dishwasher.

Stovetop Pressure Cooker : After you've clamped on the lid, you need to wait for the cooking liquid within to reach boiling point. You need to lower the heat and check the pressure buildup. You cannot leave the stove in case the pressure falls or rises too quickly. Often, you need to do this until the dish is cooked.

Then, you need to release the pressure manually. If you are doing the quick pressure release, you have to bring the cooker to the sink and run it under cold running water. If you are doing the normal release, you need to physically hold the cooker for 2 to 5 minutes while steam vents out. Only then can you release the lid.

After you've ladled out the food, you can give the bottom pan a rinse and place this in the dishwasher. Then separately wash and dry the lid by hand to prevent damaging its electronics.

Conclusion : Electric Pressure Cooker Wins!

If you still have not made up your mind about whether to buy a stovetop or an electric pressure cooker, then you might want to consider the level of your cooking expertise. Novice cooks and those with intermediate skills will learn a lot from using electric pressure cookers.

People with advanced cooking skills and cooking professionals *can* cook with stovetop cookers, but many still prefer the automatic or electric ones.

Chapter 2: Benefits Of Electric Pressure Cooking

Now that you are opting for a healthier diet, you can reap a lot by cooking more fresh food in your electronic pressure cooker. For example:

1. Cooking fresh food in the pressure cooker can preserve the integrity of the ingredients.

Quick cooking with very little moisture can help prevent food from burning, or overcooking, or turning into an unappetizing pile of mush. Your vegetables and fruits will be cooked through, but will not become limp and soggy. This is perfect for pickling and canning food as well.

2. Pressure cooking preserves the original flavors of the ingredients.

This helps lessen the use of salt, or sugar, or other flavoring agents. This is particularly helpful if you are trying to cut down on your salt and sugar intake.

3. Pressure cooking preserves the original colors of the ingredients.

The adage, *"You eat with your eyes,"* is applicable here. A colorful looking meal is easier to consume than a brownish glob of mush. If you are cooking to impress guests, or trying to entice kids to eat their veggies and fruits, this is a great way of presenting healthy but vibrant-looking meals.

4. You spend less time in the kitchen.

Using your electric pressure cooker means lessening your time preparing and cooking food by 50% to 75%. You can simply chuck in all the ingredients into one pot, close the lid, and program in the amount of pressure, cooking duration, and the type of pressure release. Your machine would do all the work for you. There is no need to watch the pot, or even be physically near the kitchen.

Cleanup is faster. After cooking, you only need to wash one pot and one lid, and both are dishwasher safe.

5. Less cooking time and quick cleaning allow you to save a lot of energy.

The kitchen remains cooler while you cook because heat does not dissipate into the surrounding air. Also, you only cook for a few minutes. Even the toughest cuts of meat can be tenderized in less than 30 minutes. Clean up is faster. This cuts down your water consumption too.

All these help keep your utility bills down. You also use less physical energy when making meals. This leaves you feeling less tired at the end of the day.

6. Pressure cooking allows you to preserve food.

Canning food (fruits, vegetables, and even meat, eggs, and fish) is far easier when you use an electric pressure cooker. You preserve all the flavors and colors of the foods, which is essential in pickling and storing them for long periods of time. You can also use your cooker to sterilize your containers (e.g. Mason jars.)

7. Using your electric pressure cooker is safer as compared to other types of cooking.

If you let your automated cooker do all the work, your chances of acquiring burns is minimal. You can leave the kitchen, and return *after* your cooker has released its pressure. There is no need to constantly watch over the pot.

Cooking Tip #4: If you are not sure how much liquid you should use in a recipe, always opt for at least 1 cup of liquid. This is the standard amount for all pressure cookers.

If at the end of the cooking cycle you find that your dish is too dry, you can always add more liquid and press the boil or sauté option on your electric pressure cooker. Press the stop button once it boils.

If you find your dish too watery, simply press the press the boil or sauté option, and leave the cooker uncovered for a few minutes. When most of the liquid has evaporated, you can press the stop button.

Chapter 3: Necessary Tools To Get You Started

Naturally, the first thing on this list would be an electric pressure cooker. Here are a few tips on how to choose one that is best suited for your kitchen.

1. Size matters.

The size of your pressure cooker determines the amount of food you can cook. Some people would advocate buying a large cooker, in case you have to cook for guests at a large party. This idea has its merits. However, unless you have a large family or a good number of people to cook for regularly, it would be best to buy a smaller, energy-efficient model.

For a household of 2 to 3, a small electric pressure cooker (about 3 to 5 quarts) would suffice. This would take up less space on your kitchen counter, consume less electricity (as compared to a larger one,) and you can cook meals faster. A smaller pot to wash is also a plus.

Here is a simple size guide for electric pressure cookers.

* 2 to 3 quarts - ideal for single servings, or 1-person meals
* 3 to 5 quarts - ideal for double portions, or for 2 to 3 people
* 6 to 8 quarts - ideal for 4 to 6 people
* 10 quarts or above - used in restaurants or households of more than
   8 people

If possible, you *should* buy pressure cookers of different sizes. This gives you the liberty to prepare a wider range of meals for any number of people. However, electric cookers take up countertop space. So a good alternative would be to buy larger or smaller stovetop cookers for those "special occasions."

If you are working on a limited budget, but would still love to cook occasionally for small parties, you can buy a small pressure cooker, and cook dishes in batches instead.

2. What are you planning to cook?
You should consider the type of food you intend to cook *regularly*. If you are living alone, but would like to have meat regularly on the menu, a better option for you would be the 3 to 5 quart pot. It has additional cooking surface for searing or browning meat. It is the perfect sized pot for making double servings of soups and stews (which you can freeze for later consumption.)

If you have a vegetarian/vegan household of 2, or you are the type who loves making soups and stews, the 6 to 8 quart pot would suit your needs nicely. This gives you larger cooking space for steaming vegetables, and you can add in a larger volume of liquid for soups. This is also ideal for cooking grains and legumes.

If you have a household of 4, but you only intend to use your electric pressure cooker to cook relatively "dry" dishes (e.g. hash browns, rice, bread, stews, etc.,) you can choose the smaller 3 to 5 quarts. A smaller pan holds less liquid, and can speed up your cooking time considerably.

If you are planning on canning or pickling regularly, you best option would be the largest pot (10 quarts or more.) This could cook a large volume of food in one go, and sterilize your pickling jars as well.

3. Your level of expertise in the kitchen.
If you are only learning how to cook, your best option would be the 6 to 8 quarts. This gives you a lot of elbow room to work with.

Also, an electric pressure cooker of this size usually has other functions (rice cooker, steamer, yogurt maker, etc.) This is the best machine to use when learning or experiment on making new dishes.

4. Your budget.
Any multi-purpose electric cooker that fits your budget is a good buy. It does not make sense to purchase a pricier model, which you are afraid to use on a regular basis. Just make sure that you

sign and send back (to the manufacturer) the product warranty. There is no need to buy an extended warranty.

5. Aluminum, enameled cast iron, or stainless steel interior?

Stainless! Although electric pressure cookers with aluminum or enameled cast iron interiors are much cheaper, stainless models are easier to clean and maintain. These do not easily dent or bend out of shape. In addition, stainless steel does not retain smells and is usually treated against rust, mold and mildew buildup.

If stainless steel is not within your budget range, enameled cast iron is a good second choice. However, this might not be the best option for sterilizing bottles (for canning or pickling.)

6. Non-stick or ceramic coating?

Non-stick coating for the interior pot is always a good thing, but ceramic non-stick coating is even better. Unfortunately, only a few manufacturers offer electric pressure cookers with ceramic coatings *that are completely non-stick*.

If you can afford the ceramic non-stick pot, then go for it. This will make cleaning up about 100 times easier.

Again, ceramic coating may not be the best thing for sterilizing bottles (for canning or pickling.)

7. Choose less complicated settings.

Some manufacturers go overboard when it comes to settings. Some machines have 30 to 40 buttons of undecipherable "programs." Instead of trying to figure these out, you can choose models with less complicated settings or fewer buttons. All you really need are:

* Timer

* *High Pressure and Low Pressure, also called Meat Setting and Rice Setting, respectively. Multi-purpose cookers have other settings, but these are the only ones you need when pressure cooking.*

Quick, normal, and natural pressure release. Never buy electric pressure cookers with only 2 types of pressure release. You would need all 3 to safely use the machine.

a. Quick pressure release brings down the internal temperature in a flash.

b. Normal or slow pressure release is more gradual. It takes a longer time, but it is safer to use if you plan on leaving the machine unattended.

c. Natural pressure release is an automatic program that releases pressure when the internal temperature is set too high. It releases short bursts of steam to ease the pressure within the cooking chamber. For stovetop pressure cookers, this function is called the "leaky lid release."

Other kitchen tools/equipment you would need (for the recipes in this book) are:

- Air tight containers
- Aluminum foil
- Baking dishes small enough to fit inside the pressure cooker for bread recipes
- Blender or food processor
- Bowls, large enough for soaking and/or mixing ingredients
- Cheese grater and/or lemon zester
- Chopping board
- Cooking and serving utensils like ladles, slotted spoons, spatula, tongs, wooden spoons, etc.
- Cutting and slicing implements like cleavers and knives
- Fork for beating eggs, fluffing up rice, testing the doneness of food, etc.
- Freezing bags or freezer safe food containers

- Kitchen towel or paper towels
- Measuring tools like measuring cups and spoons
- Microwave safe heating bowls
- Muffin or cupcake pans – individual cups (or pans,) silicone made is preferable, but disposable laminated paper cups are good alternatives. Do not use regular paper linings in electric pressure cookers, as these will wilt or fold during high pressure cooking.
- Pastry brush
- Peeler
- Saran wraps or plastic wraps
- Serving plates and/or platters
- Serving bowls, like soup bowls or ramen bowls
- Sieve or strainer
- Spice grinder, coffee grinder, or mortar and pestle
- Steamer baskets
- Wire whisk

Chapter 4: Tips For Planning Your Meals Ahead Of Time

With a busy workday, no one has the time or energy to spend hours in the kitchen. Here are a few tips on how to plan your meals using your electric pressure cooker.

1. Plan a menu for the entire week.

Knowing exactly what you want to cook or serve for the rest of the week relieves a lot of stress off your shoulders, especially on busy days. Set up a whiteboard or write down your intended meals on a planner. Try to stick to that eating plan. If you have a hard time doing so, at least have "contingency" recipes on hand for those last minute meals.

Write down your intended recipes for the week, list down individual ingredients, and the recommended amount. This will help limit your shopping expenses as well.

2. Make a shopping list. Write down the amount you need.

Sticking to your shopping list while at the store will keep you from spending too much money, time, and energy on items you don't need. More importantly, write down the exact (or approximate) amount you will need. This will help lessen waste, and you have fewer bags to carry.

3. Shop and freeze.

Buying in bulk would save you a lot of money, but if you don't know what to do with all your frozen goods, then you are wasting money instead. When you shop, buy only the things you really need *per recipe*. If the recipe indicates that you can place everything in your electric pressure cooker all at once, then:

* Prepare your ingredients,
* Place all these in a freezer bag, including the cooking liquid, if any,
* Seal the bag,

Write down what the name of the dish outside and the intended date and time you plan on cooking it, then
* Put the bag in the freezer until it is ready to use.

If the recipe has different components (e.g. you need to brown the meat or sauté a few ingredients first,) store the marinated meat or sautéing ingredients in separate bags, and the rest in one big freezer bag. Tie these together with a rubber band or string. When you pull these out of the freezer, you pull the bags out in one go.

4. Dedicate some time preparing your ingredients.

If you would rather prepare your meals fresh every time, you should dedicate about 4 hours a week (at the very least) preparing the ingredients. You don't have to do everything in one sitting, but it helps if you prepare something when you have the time.

For example:

Peel and mince garlic cloves and store these in airtight glass bottles. Place the bottle in the fridge. You can get as much or as little as you need afterwards. Crushed or minced garlic can keep in the fridge for up to 3 weeks. As reference for the recipes in this book: 1 piece garlic clove = 1 tsp. minced garlic.

Peel and mince onions. Store these in freezer bags and stick the bag in the deep freeze. This can keep in the freezer for 2 weeks. Defrost in the lower part of the fridge before using. As reference for the recipes in this book: 1 piece medium-sized onion = ½ cup minced onion; 1 piece large-sized onion = ¾ cup minced onion.

* Peel and grate ginger. Store this in the fridge as well. As reference for the recipes in this book: 1 thumb-sized piece ginger = 1 Tbsp. minced ginger.

* Marinate meats in bags whenever possible. Stick these in the coldest part of the freezer. Thaw 12 to 24 hours ahead of time by placing the bags in the lower part of the fridge.

* Prepare herbs by chopping these (or use the food processor or spice/coffee grinder,) and storing in non-reactive bottles or containers. Fill the bottles with good quality extra virgin olive oil and store in the fridge for up to 6 weeks.

* Grate hard cheeses ahead of time. Store these in non-reactive air-tight containers in the fridge for up to 4 weeks.

5. Cook and freeze.

Cooking double, triple, or quadruple servings of your favorite meal can save you a lot of time. This is particularly true if you are cooking soups and stews. You can cook a large batch in your electric pressure cooker, then divide the dish into separate portions. Place each portion in a freezer-safe, microwave-safe container, then stick it in the deep freeze.

When you are ready to eat, you can defrost and heat everything in the microwave. You could also cook and freeze broths (cooking liquids or stocks) for later use.

6. Use whatever is available in your pantry or fridge.

You do not need to rush to the grocery store every time you run out of one or two ingredients in your recipes. You can easily substitute a few with whatever is handy. For example:

* Run out of fresh parsley? Dried or powdered parsley can be used in a pinch. Fresh, dried or powdered oregano is good alternative. If nothing else, use whatever edible herb you have, but use sparingly.

* Run out of fish steaks? Try skinless chicken fillets instead. These cook a little longer, but chicken meat is quite versatile. Slicing the meat thinner and across the grain can lessen cooking time. For vegan friendly meals, try using marinated tofu.

* Run out of cream? Try any kind of broth plus fresh or canned milk instead. Your soup or stew may come out a little watery, but this can easily be resolved by reducing the liquid on the "boil" function of your electric pressure cooker. In some instances, you can even remove the cream from the recipe, and simply use broth or plain water. If you are feeling a bit adventurous and you have one at hand, use one can of coconut milk instead for every cup of cream.

Substituting a few ingredients once in a while will not really hurt your dishes. In fact, you many even "invent" a new recipe after.

7. Keep your pantry and fridge stocked with a few basic ingredients (or at least, ingredients you love using regularly.)

If you keep basic food items at hand, you can cook meals quickly. Some of the basic ingredients you should always have in your fridge or pantry include:

- Butter or any dairy substitute you want
- Cheese or any dairy substitute you want
- Canned or frozen vegetables like canned tomatoes, canned artichoke hearts, whole corn kernels, frozen peas, frozen strawberries, etc.
- Dried or powdered herbs and spices, including black or white pepper, parsley, oregano, etc.

- Eggs
- Fruits - fresh, dried, or canned
- Good quality cooking oil such as extra virgin olive oil, canola oil, coconut oil, grape seed old, etc.
- Milk or any dairy substitute you want
- Mushrooms, dried or canned are good substitutes for meat
- Uncooked rice and grains, including different kinds of pasta

Cooking Tip #5: When you prepare meals in one pot, make sure that your ingredients are sliced in almost the same sizes or shapes. This makes your cooked dishes look visually appetizing, and makes for fast and even cooking.

Chapter 5: Common Mistakes To Avoid

Don't : overload your cooker with food or liquid.
Placing too much food or cooking liquid inside your electric pressure cooker will only delay cooking time. This will greatly affect the boiling temperature within, and the pressure build up.
Do : fill your cooker only half full if you are cooking a relatively dry dish. If you are cooking soups and stew, you can fill your cooker 2/3 full.

Don't : place frozen meat inside the cooker.
Your electric pressure cooker will take a long time to reach boiling temperature if you have a large chunk of frozen meat inside it. This will prolong cooking time, and may cause uneven cooking.
Do : thaw the meat completely in the fridge first for 12 to 24 hours. If the meat is marinated, thawing would only improve its taste. If you are using beef, pork or chicken meat, it would be best to brown these to bring out their flavor. Note: browning means lightly fry the meat in oil until the cut sides have a thin patina of color.
The same goes for broths, or other liquids you will use for cooking (e.g. milk, cream, tomato sauce, etc.) Thaw these out first.
You can place frozen vegetables and fruits safely inside an electric pressure cooker, as these usually cook faster than meat.
Don't : assume that all food cook faster on high pressure.
Meats, soups and stews can survive high pressure cooking, but not delicate food items like seafood, fruits and leafy vegetables.
Do : take the time to look at the recipes and remember which ones can be cooked on high pressure and which ones on low pressure.

Some food items *must* be cooked on low pressure at a very short time.

Cooking Tip #6: When cooking with beans, grains and legumes (rice, peas, quinoa, kidney beans, mung beans, lentils, etc.,) fill your pot only halfway up or less. These food items usually develop a thick foam or grainy "bubbles" when subjected to high heat. Unfortunately, the foam can also escape through the pressure vent, and spill all over the kitchen counter. If you want to cook a large volume of beans, grains and legumes, try cooking these in batches.

Don't : stop the cooking cycle for any reason.
An electric pressure cooker works best when left on its own. If you stop its cooking cycle for any reason at all, or override its pre-programmed settings, you not only compromise the quality of your food, but you also increase your risk of getting burns by intentionally releasing the pressure inside. This practice also damages the durability of the machine.

Do : lessen the cooking time by half.
If you have reservations about internal temperature or pressure, or would like to check the meat *at least once in the middle of a cooking cycle,* it would be best to shorten the cooking time by half. This allows the machine to bring the pressure down naturally. You can check your dish safely at this point, then start the cycle again.

Don't : let your electric pressure cooker go on indefinitely.
An electric pressure cooker does not have the same function as that of a slow cooker. You can easily burn food if you let it run for a long period of time. Electric pressure cookers work best with "flash" cooking (30 minutes or less,) for relatively dry dishes. Soups, or any dish that has more than 3 cups of cooking liquid can be cooked for up to an hour.

Do : set a timer when cooking with pressure cookers.

To avoid burning food, and to maintain the integrity of the machine, always set a timer when cooking with an electric pressure cooker.

Make sure also that you set the type of pressure release. So when the timer goes off, the machine automatically releases pressure. This reduces the risk of overcooking or burning your food.

Don't : ever attempt the cold water - quick pressure release on an electric pressure cooker.

Subjecting your electrical appliance to water can permanently damage the machine. Worse still, it could explode and cause you physical harm.

Do : use the quick release option on the machine instead.

The quick release option allows the pressure to be released quickly, without the need for running water. This may take longer (as compared to its stovetop counterpart,) but is 100% safer.

Don't : put the entire machine in the dishwasher.

Again, you should avoid subjecting electric appliances to running water.

Do : place only the interior cooking pot and lid in the dishwasher.

The rest of the machine would benefit from a regular wipe down with a clean but dry cloth. Make sure the pressure cooker is unplugged before cleaning it.

Cooking Tip #7: Fresh and frozen ingredients always cook longer than canned ones. If you are substituting mostly canned food items for fresh or frozen produce (especially for fruits and vegetables like blueberries or green peas,) try to lessen the cooking time of the dish or opt for low pressure cooking instead.

Chapter 6: Easy Pressure Cooker Breakfast Recipes

Very Important Note: Always check the psi (pressure per square inch) of your electric pressure cooker. The rule is: the lower the psi (lower than 15 psi,) the longer the cooking time. Adjust your timer accordingly. This applies to all the recipes in this book.

Recipe #1 : Apple, Berry and Nuts Risotto

Preparation Time : 10 minutes
Cooking Time : 6 minutes
Serves:4
Ingredients :

- 2 Tbsp. butter or margarine. For a dairy-free dish, you can
- substitute any lightly-flavored cooking oil.
- 1 ½cups Arborio rice, or any long-grained rice of your choice.
- rinsed until water runs clear, drained well.
- To remove the gluten, you can substitute quinoa, or other non-gluten, low GI (Glycemic Index) grain
- 2 pieces apples, large-sized, cored, diced into bite-sized pieces,
- soaked in …
- 1 cup apple juice
- 1/3cup brown sugar, or any natural sweetener of your choice
- ¼tsp. sea salt or kosher salt
- 1 ½tsp.cinnamon powder
- 3cups milk of your choice (e.g. skim, 1%, or soy) Add more, if
- desired. For a dairy-free dish, you can substitute apple
- juice.
- ½ cup dried berries of your choice e.g. blueberries, cherries,
- raspberries, etc. You can also substitute other dried
- fruits like dates and mangoes.
- ½ cups honey roasted cashew nuts. Toasted almonds and
- walnuts also work well in this recipe. You can remove
- this ingredient if you have peanut or nut allergy.

Directions:

1. Set the electric pressure cooker on high pressure without the lid on. Melt the butter in the cooking pot.
2. Add in the rice and stir often. Coat the individual rice grains with the butter. Continue stirring until most of the grains are opaque, about 4 to 5 minutes.

Note: if your electric pressure cooker does not have a sauté function, you can do steps 1 and 2 on a separate pot on the stovetop. Transfer the lightly cooked rice into the pressure cooker after, then continue with the next steps. This applies to the rest of the recipes in this book.

3. Add in the apples, brown sugar, cinnamon and salt.
4. Pour in the apple juice and milk.
5. Give the rice mix a final stir and clamp on the lid. Select high pressure and cook for 6 minutes with the quick pressure release option.
6. After the pressure release, leave the risotto inside the cooker for at least a minute more. This lets the rice reabsorb the cooking liquid. Do not remove the lid.
7. Stir in the dried berries and nuts after. Add more milk, if desired. Serve warm.

Recipe #2 : Gluten-Free Egg Muffins

Preparation Time : 10 minutes
Cooking Time : 8 minutes
Serves:4
Equipment Needed : steamer basket that would fit inside the pressure
cooker; 4 silicon baking/muffin cups, or you can use
individual muffin tins lined with laminated
baking paper; rubber spatula
Ingredients :

- 1 ½cupswater for steaming
- 4 pieces eggs, large-sized
- ¼tsp.fresh lemon zest
- ½ tsp. lemon juice
- 1 pinch dried chili flakes
- 1 dash black pepper, or to taste
- 1 piecescallion, roots trimmed off, use the white part only,
- sliced thinly diagonally
- 4 Tbsp.cheddar or any hard cheese of your choice. You can
- substitute cashew butter or flavored tofu to make this
- dairy-free.
- 4slices cooked bacon, crumbled. You can substitute any
- cooked protein source of your choice, or remove this
- ingredient for a more vegan/vegetarian-friendly dish
- sea salt or kosher salt, to taste

Directions:

1.Place the steamer basket with the 1½ cups water inside the pressure cooker. Set the cooker on high pressure. Let the water come to a boil. Turn down the heat to the lowest setting but do not put the lid on.

2.Meanwhile, crack the eggs into a separate bowl. Add in the black pepper, lemon zest, lemon juice, and the dried chili flakes. Mix until eggs are frothy.

3.Divide the bacon, cheese and scallions evenly between the silicon muffin cups. Pour the same amount of egg mixture into each cup. Using a fork, gently stir the ingredients together.

4.Carefully place all 4 muffin tins in the steamer basket. Clamp on the lid. Select high pressure, and let the eggs cook for 8 minutes, with the quick pressure release option.

5.After 8 minutes, immediately turn off the heat, but keep the lid on for another 2 minutes.

6.After the allotted time, carefully lift out the steamer basket. Remove the muffin tins.

7.Using a rubber spatula, carefully pry loose the cooked egg muffins. You can serve these as they are if you are using the laminated paper cups. Serve warm.

Recipe #3 : Potatoes and Sweet Potatoes Hash Browns

Preparation Time : 30 minutes
Cooking Time : 7 minutes
Serves:4
Equipment Needed : peeler; kitchen towel; fine sieve or strainer;
food processor or grater; spatula; paper towels
Ingredients :

- ½ kg baking sweet potatoes (e.g. New Jewell or Yellow
- Jersey or Bunch,) washed, skins peeled thinly, then
- soaked in cold water to prevent browning
- ½ kg russet or Yukon potatoes, washed, skins peeled thinly,
- then soaked in cold water to prevent browning
- 2 Tbsp. olive oil
- ½tsp. dried oregano leaves, not the powdered kind, roughly
- chopped
- ½tsp. dried parsley leaves, not the powdered kind, roughly
- chopped
- ¾cup crumbled cooked bacon. You can substitute any
- cooked protein source of your choice, e.g. turkey
- Bacon or fried tofu skins. You can also remove this
- ingredient if you prefer a vegan/vegetarian-friendly
- meal.
- sea salt or kosher salt, to taste
- white pepper, to taste

Direction:

1. Remove sweet potatoes from its soaking liquid. Grate or process the sweet potatoes until these come out in fine threads. If you are using a food processor, take care not to turn these into liquid mush. Do the same for the potatoes.

2. Place the grated potatoes and sweet potatoes into the fine sieve or strainer. Run cold water over the threads for at least 30 seconds to remove most of the starch. Using your hands, gather these into a ball and squeeze out most of the water.

3. Transfer to a clean and dry kitchen towel. Gently spread the threads apart, while blotting out the excess water. The less moisture your potatoes and sweet potatoes have, the crunchier your hash browns will be.

4. Meanwhile, set the cooker on high pressure. Pour in the olive oil and wait until the oil starts to smoke slightly, about 1 minute.

5. Place the processed potatoes and sweet potatoes into the hot oil. Gently sauté until most of the threads have turned golden brown. This would take about 3 to 5 minutes, depending on your pressure cooker's psi.

6. Add in the bacon, oregano and parsley. Mix well.

Note: if your pressure cooker does not have a sauté function, you can do steps 4, 5 and 6 on a non-stick skillet on the stovetop. Transfer the partially cooked potatoes and sweet potatoes to the pressure cooker afterwards.

7. Using the back of your spoon or spatula, press down on the potato and sweet potato threads until these cover most of the cooking surface of the pressure cooker. Clamp on the lid.

8. Select low pressure cooking, for 7 minutes. Select the quick release option.

9. After the pressure is released, remove the lid. Using a spatula, lift out the hash and place on a paper towel-lined plate. Season lightly with salt and pepper. Serve while hot.

Recipe #4 : Quinoa with Brown Rice "Cereal"

Preparation Time : 10 minutes
Cooking Time : 12 minutes
Serves:4
Ingredients :

1cup brown rice (or any dark colored, low GI rice substitute of your choice)

1 cup red quinoa

2 Tbsp. coconut oil, or any mild tasting oil

5 ½cupswater

1 pinchsea salt or kosher salt

¼ cup agave sugar or any natural sugar substitute of your choice

¼cupraisins, or any dried or fresh fruits of your choice

¼ cupmilk (optional)

Directions:
1. Place both the quinoa and the brown rice in a strainer and rinse under cold running water. Stop when the water runs clear. Drain well.

2. Set up the sauté function of your electric pressure cooker. Heat the oil until slightly smoky, about 1 minute.

3.Place in the well-drained rice and quinoa. Sauté until the individual grains are lightly coated with oil. Mix until some of the rice have turned opaque, about 2 to 3 minutes.

4.Carefully pour in the water and mix gently. Add in the sea salt, sugar and raisins. Clamp on the lid, and cook on high pressure for 12 minutes, with the normal pressure release option.

5.Remove the lid after the pressure has been released. Using a fork, gently fluff up the rice and quinoa. Serve warm with milk, if desired.

Recipe #5 : Tea Eggs

Preparation Time : 10 minutes
Cooking Time : 15 minutes
Serves:4
Equipment Needed : steamer basket
Ingredients :

4 pieces eggs, large-sized, hard-boiled, shells lightly cracked all over but not removed, cooled to room temperature

¼ cup light soy sauce

1 piece lemon, zests only

2 tea bags black tea

1 Tbsp. dried cloves, whole

1 Tbsp. black peppercorns, whole

1 Tbsp. juniper berries

2 pieces bay leaves, whole

1 cupwater

Directions:

1.Prepare your electric pressure cooker by pouring in the lemon zest, cloves, peppercorns, juniper berries, tea bags and the water. Add in the soy sauce and mix gently.

2.In the meantime, place the cracked hard boiled eggs into the steamer basket. Lower the basket into the pressure cooker pot.

Clamp on the lid and set on low pressure for 15 minutes, with the normal pressure release option.

3. After the pressure has been released, carefully remove the eggs and let to cool to room temperature. Discard the cooking liquid.

4. Once the eggs have cooled completely, remove the shells. The eggs should have that marbled look. Serve the eggs whole. Tea eggs are also good served slightly chilled.

Recipe #6 : Raisin Bread Pudding with Salted Caramel

Preparation Time : 30 minutes
Cooking Time : 16 minutes for the salted caramel;
20 minutes for bread pudding
Serves:4
Equipment Needed : glass or metal baking dish with tall sides, which can
hold approximately 1 to 1 ½ quarts of liquid, small
enough to fit inside the pressure cooker;
aluminum foil; steamer basket; pastry brush
Ingredients :

For the bread

4 Tbsp. butter, melted

½ cup brown sugar, packed

3 cups whole milk, or any milk substitute of choice

3 pieces eggs, large-sized, beaten

1 tsp.vanilla

½ tsp. cinnamon powder

¼ tsp.sea salt or kosher salt

7 piecesraisin bread, thick-sliced, cubed. You can substitute any kind of thick-sliced bread of your choice.

½cup raisins

1 ½cupswater, for steaming

butter, at room temperature, for greasing

For the salted caramel sauce

1cup white sugar, packed

6Tbsp. compound (also called salted) butter, cubed

½cupheavy cream

1 tsp. sea salt

Directions:

For the salted caramel sauce

1. On the boil function of your electric pressure cooker, place the white sugar into the pot.

2. Using a rubber spatula, constantly stir the sugar until it liquefies and turns amber-colored, about 10 to 15 minutes. Be careful not to burn the sugar.

3. Add the butter and stir vigorously.

4. Drizzle in the heavy cream while mixing vigorously.

5. Once all the cream is added, let the caramel boil for one minute, before sprinkling in the sea salt.

6. Turn off the pressure cooker. Carefully transfer the salted caramel sauce into a heat-resistant container and allow to cool completely at room temperature before using.

Note: you can do this beforehand. The salted caramel sauce will keep well outside the fridge for 1 week.

For the raisin bread pudding

1. In a large mixing bowl, combine the brown sugar, melted butter, milk, eggs, vanilla, salt, and cinnamon powder. Mix until frothy. Fold in the raisins and cubed bread. Make sure the bread is well soaked.

2. Using a pastry brush, grease the sides and bottom of the baking dish with a thin layer of butter. Pour the pudding mix into the baking dish only 2/3 full. Cover with aluminum or tin foil.

3. Meanwhile, prepare the pressure cooker by adding in the water. Place baking dish in the middle of the steamer basket, then lower the latter into the pressure cooker.

4. Clamp on the lid, and set on high pressure for 20 minutes, with the quick pressure release option.

5. Once the pressure is released, carefully remove the steamer basket from the cooker and remove the baking dish.

6. Scoop out one serving per person, and pour a tablespoon of salted caramel sauce. Add more, if desired. Serve warm.

Recipe #7 : Fluffy Scrambled Eggs

Preparation Time : 10 minutes
Cooking Time : 2 minutes
Serves:4
Equipment Needed : mixing bowl; whisk; pastry brush
Ingredients :

4 pieces eggs, large-sized, whites separated, yolks set aside

½ cup fresh milk, or any dairy substitute of your choice

1 Tbsp. extra virgin olive oil

pinch salt

pinch white pepper

Directions:

1.Prepare the pressure cooking by setting it on high pressure. Using the pastry brush, lightly grease the bottom and sides of the cooking pot with the olive oil.

2.In a small bowl, mix together the egg yolks and milk. Season well with salt and pepper.

3.In a larger mixing bowl, vigorously beat the egg whites firmly until peaks develop, about 5 to 7 minutes.

4.Gently fold in the egg-milk mixture. Make sure that you do not remove all the air from the egg whites. Transfer this quickly in the heated pressure cooker pot.

5.Clamp on the lid and set the timer for 2 minutes. Set this on the quick pressure release.

6.When the pressure is released, carefully remove the scrambled egg from the pot and divide into 4. Serve immediately.

Recipe #8 : Hungarian Sausage Omelet

Preparation Time : 15 minutes
Cooking Time : 7 minutes
Serves:4
Equipment Needed : mixing bowl; whisk; pastry brush; rubber spatula
Ingredients :

4 pieces eggs, large-sized, beaten well until frothy

1 piece smoked Hungarian sausage, diced. You can substitute any other kind of smoked sausage for this recipe.

½ cup fresh milk, or any dairy substitute of your choice

½ cup freshly grated Romano cheese or any hard cheese of your choice

1 Tbsp. extra virgin olive oil

1 tsp. white wine vinegar (or any vinegar of your choice)

salt, to taste

white pepper, to taste

Directions:

1.In a small bowl, mix together the eggs, cheese, and milk. Season lightly with salt and pepper. Set aside.

2.Prepare the pressure cooking by setting it on high pressure. Pour in the oil and the diced sausage. Using a rubber spatula, sauté the sausage bits until most have turned golden, about 5 minutes. Remove the partially cooked sausage to a plate.

3. Deglaze the cooking surface by pouring in the white wine vinegar. Scrape the bottom gently. Return the sausage bits to the cooking pot. Pour in the egg mix, and give the dish a final stir.

4. Clamp on the lid and set the cooker on high pressure for 2 minutes with the quick pressure release option.

5. Once cooked, carefully remove the omelet from the pot and divide into 4. Serve plain or with rice or bread.

Recipe #9 : Easy Mushroom Soup in the Morning

Preparation Time : 5 minutes
Cooking Time : 2 minutes
Serves:4
Ingredients :

1cansliced button mushrooms, rinsed under running water, drained well

2cupsvegetable broth

¼cup frozen peas

salt, to taste

black pepper, to taste

1 piece egg yolk (optional)

Directions:

1. Place the mushrooms, frozen peas and vegetable broth into the pressure cooking. Clamp on the lid. Set this on high pressure for 2 minutes with the quick pressure release option.

2. Carefully remove the lid and drop in the egg yolk (if using.) Let the soup sit undisturbed for about 1 minute. This would cook the outside of the egg yolk, but its center should still be runny.

3. Season with salt and pepper just before serving. Serve warm. This is best served with saltines, or toasted bread.

Recipe #10 : Breakfast Chocolate Drink (Kiddie Version)

Preparation Time : 5 minutes
Cooking Time : 4 minutes
Serves:4
Ingredients :

4Tbsp.good quality breakfast cocoa

25 grams milk chocolate, chopped into smaller pieces

25 gramswhite chocolate, chopped into smaller pieces

4 cups fresh milk, or any milk substitute of your choice

1 Tbsp.brown sugar

 pinch sea salt or kosher salt

4 tsp. marshmallows, for sprinkling (optional)

Directions:

1.Except for the marshmallows, place all the ingredients into the pressure cooker.

2.Clamp on the lid. Set this on high pressure, for 4 minutes, with the quick pressure release option.

3.Once the chocolate drink is cooked, allow this to cool for at least 2 minutes before ladling into individual cups.

4.Top off with marshmallows, if desired. Serve immediately.

Recipe #11 : Breakfast Chocolate Drink (Adult Version)

Preparation Time : 7 minutes
Cooking Time : 4 minutes
Serves:4
Ingredients :

4Tbsp.good quality breakfast cocoa

1 Tbsp. instant coffee of your choice

25 grams dark or bitter chocolate, chopped into smaller pieces

4 cups fresh milk, or any milk substitute of your choice

1 Tbsp.brown sugar

 pinch sea salt or kosher salt

4 pieces Amaretto cookies, crumbled by hand, for sprinkling (optional) Note: if you have peanut allergy, you can substitute wafer cookies instead.

Directions:

1.Except for the Amaretto cookies, place all the ingredients into the pressure cooker.

2.Clamp on the lid. Set this on high pressure, for 4 minutes, with the quick pressure release option.

3.Once the chocolate drink is cooked, allow the beverage to cool for at least 5 minutes before ladling into individual cups.

4.Top off with the crushed cookies, if desired.

Recipe #12 : Pot Torte with Frozen Fruit Sauce

Preparation Time : 45 minutes
Cooking Time : 14 minutes for the sauce; 10 minutes for the torte
Serves:4
Ingredients :

For the torte

½ cup all-purpose flour, sifted twice. You can substitute ¼ cup all-purpose flour plus ¼ cup whole wheat flour. Do not use cake flour.

 pinch sea salt or kosher salt

2 Tbsp. white sugar

¼ tsp. baking powder

¼ tsp. ground nutmeg

½ cup milk, or plain water to make this dairy-free

1 piece egg, beaten until frothy

¼ tsp. vanilla

¼ tsp. melted butter, or any mild tasting oil to make this dairy-free

melted butter, or any mild tasting oil, for greasing

For the frozen fruit sauce

1 cup frozen strawberries, or any berries of your choice

1 cup frozen blueberries, or any berries of your choice

1 cup sugar

1 cup water

For the garnish

2 pieces frozen bananas, peeled and roughly chopped

½ cup frozen grapes, preferably seedless, quartered
Directions:

To make the frozen fruit sauce

1. Place all the ingredients of the frozen fruit sauce into the pressure cooker. Stir until sugar and fruits are well combined. Slightly bruise or crush the berries to help these release their juices faster.

2. Clamp on the lid. Set this on high pressure, for 4 minutes, with the quick pressure release option.

3. Once the pressure is released, press the boil function so as to reduce the volume of the sauce by half, about 10 minutes.

4. When the sauce has been reduced, turn off the pressure cooker and carefully ladle out the sauce into a heat resistant container. Allow the sauce to cool completely at room temperature before storing in the freezer.

Ideally, this should be frozen for at least an hour before using. But you can use the sauce lightly chilled for at least 15 minutes. This will keep fresh in the freezer for up to for 3 days.

For the torte

1. Lightly grease the pressure cooker's pot with butter. Make sure you grease the bottom and sides well.

2. Combine the dry ingredients into a large bowl: flour, salt, sugar, nutmeg and baking powder.

3. In a separate bowl, whisk the eggs with the milk until frothy. Add in the vanilla and melted butter. Mix well.

4. Combine the dry and wet ingredients. Mix until lumps in the batter have disappeared.

7. Pour the batter into the pressure cooker and clamp on the lid. Set on low pressure for 10 minutes, with the quick release option.

8. Once cooked, remove the lid and allow the torte to cool completely at room temperature. This would make it easier to pry the cake out of the cooking pot.

To assemble

1. Slice the torte into 4 equal portions. Place each portion on individual serving plates.

2. Divide the frozen grapes and bananas equally among the serving plates.

3. Ladle as much (or as little) of the fruit sauce. Serve immediately.

Recipe #13 : Cheesy Cauliflower Pops

Preparation Time : 20 minutes
Cooking Time : 10 minutes
Serves:3 minutes
Equipment Needed : steamer basket
Ingredients :

1head cauliflower, trimmed, washed and drained well, sliced into bite-sized florets. You can substitute broccoli. Brussels sprouts also work well with this recipe.

2 cupswater, for steaming

salt, to taste

1 cup Buffalo mozzarella, drained well, torn roughly by hand into bite-sized pieces (optional)

Directions:

1.Lightly season the cauliflower florets with salt. Tumble these into the steamer basket.

2.Place the water into the pressure cooker, followed by the steamer basket.

3.Clamp on the lid and set on high pressure for 3 minutes, with the quick release option.

4.After 3 minutes, remove the lid. If using, sprinkle the shredded mozzarella on top of the cooked cauliflower florets and close the lid once more. Let the dish sit undisturbed for 2 minutes, or until most of the cheese has melted.

5.Divide the dish into 4 equal portions. Serve warm.

Recipe #14 : Faux Pho

Preparation Time : 20 minutes
Cooking Time : 10 minutes
Serves:4
Ingredients :

1handful dried rice noodles, thick cut, broken into manageable pieces (or would at least fit into the cooking pot.)
Approximately 2 cups uncooked noodles, or 1 cup cooked noodles. You can substitute linguini, lasagnette, or tagliatelle. In a pinch, you can use any flat, dried, and fast cooking noodles or pasta.

2 cups water

2 cups vegetable or chicken broth

1 cup cooked boiled or roasted chicken, pork or beef, sliced thinly or shredded, bones and skins removed
Leftovers are fine. If you prefer fresher ingredients,
you can substitute ½ cup cubed fish grouper or tilapia filets or shrimps. For a more vegan fare, cubed extra firm tofu works well with this recipe too.

½ tsp. light soy sauce

½tsp.fish sauce

1 tsp. brown sugar, or any sweetener of your choice

1 tsp. chili flakes, or hot pepper flakes

½ tsp. garlic powder

½ tsp.onion powder

¼ tsp. ginger powder

dash Spanish paprika

dashblack pepper

1piece lemongrass, use the white part only, roots and green leaves trimmed off, crush the white part, leave whole

1 piece dried star anise, whole

1piecebird's eye chili, stem trimmed, halved, seeds removed
You can substitute any fresh chili of your choice

1 Tbsp. frozen or canned whole kernel corn

1 Tbsp.frozen diced carrot

¼ head white cabbage, washed, drained well, roughly chopped

2 leaves napa cabbage, washed, drained well, center stems removed, roughly chopped

For the garnish

handfulfresh cilantro (coriander,) roughly chopped,

salt, to taste

drops sesame sauce

4 pieces hard boiled eggs, shelled, kept warm (optional)

Directions:

1. Except for the garnishes, place all the ingredients into the pressure cooker pot.

2. Select high pressure for 10 minutes, with the quick release option.

3. Once the soup is cooked, try to scoop out the whole lemongrass and star anise. Discard.

4. Taste the soup and add salt, if needed.

5. Ladle the soup into 4 individual cups. Sprinkle with a little cilantro and a few drops of sesame oil on top. Just before serving, add in one whole egg per cup, if desired. Serve warm.

Recipe #15 : Breadless Sausage Burger

Preparation Time : 10 minutes
Cooking Time : 10 minutes
Serves:4
Ingredients :

1/2pound fresh Italian sausage, meat removed from casings, You can substitute any fresh sausage for this recipe.

2 pieces white onions, large-sized, peeled and minced

1 handful parsley, finely chopped

½ cup oats (rolled, instant, or old-fashioned can be used)

1 piece egg

1 Tbsp. tomato paste

1 Tbsp. extra virgin olive oil

extra virgin olive oil, for brushing

For serving:

(as much as you want) bed of lettuce

(as much as you want) chopped tomatoes

 drizzle yellow or English mustard (optional)

Directions:

1. With a pastry brush, oil the bottom and sides of the cooking pot. Set aside.

2. In a large mixing bowl, combine all the remaining ingredients together (except the lettuce and tomatoes) until most of the oats have been fully incorporated into the meat. Transfer the sausage mix into the prepared cooking pot.

3. Using the back of the spoon or spatula, gently press down the sausage mix so that it forms a relatively large, but flat looking burger patty.

4. Pierce the patty with a fork to let the juices of the burger escape while cooking.
5. Clamp on the lid. Set the pressure cooker on high pressure for 10 minutes, with the quick release option.

6. After the pressure is released, turn off the pressure cooker, but do not remove the lid. Let the burger rest for at least 2 minutes. This step allows the meat to reabsorb most of its cooking juices.

7. After 2 minutes, remove the lid. Divide the patty into 4, using a rubber spatula. Spoon out individual "patties" and serve each on a bed of fresh lettuce leaves and tomatoes. Drizzle with a little mustard, desired.

Recipe #16 : Easy Cheesy Chicken Salad

Preparation Time : 30 minutes
Cooking Time : 10 minutes
Serves:4
Ingredients :

For the chicken broth

½ pound chicken thigh fillets, skins removed, washed, pat dried

2 tsp. good quality fish sauce

 dashwhite pepper

 dash Spanish paprika

1 tsp. sugar

1 piece carrot, unpeeled, halved

1 piece leek, washed, roots removed, sliced into 4 inch long slivers

1 stem celery, washed, end removed, sliced into 4 inch long Slivers

½ piece bell pepper, cored, deseeded, quartered

2 cups water

For the salad

2cupselbow macaroni or any kind of small pasta shells, like conchigliette, lumache or rotini, cooked according to package instructions, drained well, oiled lightly to prevent pasta from sticking together, and cooled completely at room temperature. You can cook this beforehand.

4 Tbsp. plain mayo, or any mayonnaise substitute you want

1 Tbsp. yellow mustard

½ cup cheddar cheese, diced into bite-size pieces, or approximately the same size as that of the cooked chicken

¼ cup fresh celery, minced

¼ cup raisins

salt, to taste

pepper, to taste

bed of crisp lettuce

saltines (optional)

Directions:

1. Place all the ingredients of the chicken broth into the pressure cooker pot. Set on high pressure for 10 minutes, with the quick pressure release option.

2. When the pressure is released, remove the chicken fillets from the cooking liquid. You can use the reserved liquid as soup stock in other dishes.

3.Let the chicken fillets cool slightly. Dice the meat into bite-sized pieces.

4.In a large bowl, toss in all the ingredients of the salad, along with the chicken meat. Season with salt and pepper, if needed.

5.You can serve this immediately on a bed of lettuce. Or, you can chill the salad in the fridge for at least half an hour. Serve with saltines, if desired.

Recipe #17 : Corned Beef Hash

Preparation Time : 15 minutes
Cooking Time : 17 to 20 minutes
Serves:4
Ingredients :

2 Tbsp.olive oil, or any mild flavored cooking oil

1 tsp. crushed garlic

1 piecewhite onion, peeled, minced

½piece bell pepper, cored, minced

2 pieces plum ripe tomatoes, medium-sized, halved, deseeded, minced

2 pieces baking potatoes, washed, peeled, minced
8ounces cooked corned beef, roughly chopped

1 cup water

For the garnish

4 pieces eggs, cooked sunny side up, or cooked however which way you prefer

2 Tbsp. chopped parsley

salt, to taste

Directions:

1.Set the cooker on high pressure, with the lid removed. Place in the oil and heat until slightly smoky, about 1 minute.

2.Place in the onions and garlic. Sauté until onions are transparent, about 3 minutes. Take care not to burn the garlic.

3.Add in the tomatoes and bell pepper. Continue cooking for about 2 minutes.

4.Toss in the potatoes, corned beef and water. Mix well.

5.Clamp on the lid. Cook for 12 minutes with the quick release option.

6.When the pressure is released, remove the lid. If the corned beef is a little watery, continue cooking uncovered for 3 minutes. If not, you can serve this immediately.

To assemble:

1.Divide the corned beef hash into 4 equal portions.

2.Serve each portion on a plate, with one cooked egg apiece on top or on the side.

3.Sprinkle the chopped cilantro on top. Serve while warm.

Recipe #18 : Smoked Salmon on Scrambled Eggs

Preparation Time : 10 minutes
Cooking Time : 5 minutes
Serves:4
Ingredients :

8 pieces eggs, large-sized, beaten well until frothy

1 cup cream, or any cream substitute of your choice. Plain water, or low sodium vegetable broth can also be used as a substitute, to make this a dairy-free dish.

½ tsp. lemon zest

2 Tbsp. fresh lemon juice, approximately, the juice of a quarter of a lemon

¼ cup smoked salmon, roughly chopped

salt, to taste

white pepper, to taste

extra virgin olive oil, for greasing

For the garnish

2 Tbsp. fresh chives, roots and yellow leaves removed, washed well, minced, divided into 4 equal portions

lemon wedges

Directions:

1. Using a pastry brush, grease the bottom and sides of the cooking surface of the pressure cooker.
2. Combine the cream, lemon zest and lemon juice in a small mixing bowl. Season with salt and pepper. Mix until the cream thickens a little.
3. Pour in the beaten eggs and mix vigorously.
4. Pour egg-cream mixture into the prepared pot. Sprinkle in the chopped smoked salmon.
5. Set the pressure cooker on high for 5 minutes, with the quick release option.
6. Once the omelet is cooked, spoon out equal portions on a plate. Sprinkle the chopped chives on top just before serving. Place a lemon wedge on the side.

Recipe #19 : French Toast Pudding with Choco Hazelnut

Preparation Time : 20 minutes
Cooking Time : 5 minutes
Serves:4
Ingredients :

8 slices white bread, preferably thick-sliced

2 pieces eggs, beaten until frothy

2 cupsfresh milk

¼ tsp. vanilla

¼ tsp. nutmeg powder

2 pieces overripe bananas, peeled, thickly sliced

4 Tbsp. chocolate hazelnut spread, at room temperature, divided into 4 equalportions. You can substitute plain chocolate spread if you have peanut allergy.

butter, or any mild tasting oil, for greasing
For garnish
whipped cream (optional)

Directions:
1.Using a pastry brush, grease the bottom and sides of the cooking surface of the pressure cooker.

2.Combine the eggs, milk, vanilla and nutmeg in a mixing bowl. Mix well.

3. Take 2 slices of the white bread and soak these, one after the other in the egg-milk mixture.

4. Place both slices on the bottom of the pressure cooker, taking care to cover as much cooking surface as possible. Do not press down on the soaked bread, so that the pudding comes out fluffy, instead of flat.

If your pressure cooker is too small, tear off portions of the soaked bread, and reserve the rest for another layer.

If your pressure cooker is too large, add one more soaked bread slice to the pot.

5. Add a layer of sliced bananas on top of the soaked bread.

6. Repeat steps #3, #4 and #5 until you have used up all the bananas and bread slices. The topmost layer should be the soaked bread.

7. Pour in the rest of the egg-milk mix into the pot.

8. Clamp on the lid. Set the cooker on high pressure for 5 minutes, with the quick release option.

9. After 5 minutes, remove the lid. Divide the dish into 4 equal portions and spoon each portion on a plate.

10. Top off each portion with a tablespoon each of the chocolate hazelnut spread.

11. Serve with whipped cream, if desired.

Recipe #20 : French Toast Pudding with Nuts and Jam

Preparation Time : 25 minutes
Cooking Time : 5 minutes
Serves:4
Ingredients :

6 or 7 slices egg-free, dairy-free bread, preferably thick-sliced. The number of bread slices would depend on the size of your pressure cooker.

2 cupsapple juice

2 Tbsp.honey, or any liquid, natural sweetener of your choice

¼ tsp. cinnamon powder

4 Tbsp. raisins

4 Tbsp. honey roasted cashews, roughly chopped

4 Tbsp. apricot jam, divided into 4 equal portions. You can substitute any other fruit jam of your choice.

canola or coconut oil, for greasing
For garnish
whole mint leaves, washed and dried, at least one leafper serving (optional)
 drizzle honey (optional)

Directions:
1.Using a pastry brush, grease the bottom and sides of the cooking surface of the pressure cooker.

2. Combine the apple juice, honey, and cinnamon powder in a mixing bowl. Mix well.

3. Take 2 slices of the white bread and soak these, one after the other in the seasoned apple juice mix.

4. Place both slices on the bottom of the pressure cooker, taking care to cover as much cooking surface as possible. Do not press down on the soaked bread.

5. Add a layer of cashew nuts on top of the soaked bread.

6. Repeat steps #3, and #4.

7. Add a layer of raisins.

8. Add the final layer of soaked bread.

9. Pour in the rest of the seasoned apple juice mix into the pot.

10. Clamp on the lid. Set the cooker on high pressure for 5 minutes, with the quick release option.

11. After 5 minutes, remove the lid. Divide the dish into 4 equal portions and spoon each portion on a plate.

12. Top off each portion with a tablespoon each of apricot jam.

13. Serve with mint leaves. Drizzle with honey, if desired.

Chapter 7: Simple Pressure Cooker Lunch Recipes

Recipe #21 : Pasta Pasticciata (A Mess of Pasta)

Preparation Time : 25 minutes
Cooking Time : 13 to 15 minutes
Serves:4
Ingredients :

1 cup uncooked salad macaroni, or any other small macaroni of your choice like mezzemaniche, penne, or rigatoni

¼ pound lean ground beef, or any ground meat of your choice

1 piece garlic clove, peeled, minced

1 piece white onion, peeled, minced

1 stalk celery, roots trimmed, tough fibers removed, minced

1 piece carrot, small-sized, top removed, unpeeled, minced

1 cup tomato sauce

1 Tbsp.tomato paste

1 cup red wine

1 Tbsp. white sugar

2 tsp. sea salt or kosher salt

1 tsp. dried chili flakes

1tsp. white pepper

1 Tbsp.extra virgin olive oil

For the garnish

freshly grated parmigiano reggiano, or any hard cheese of your choice

Directions:

1. Pour the olive oil into the pressure cooker's pot. Set it on high pressure. Wait until the oil starts to smoke a little, about 1 minute.

2. With the lid off, sauté the onions and the garlic until aromatic, about 2 minutes.

3. Add in the ground beef and brown the meat all over. This should take about 5 to 7 minutes, depending on how high your machine's psi is.

4. When the meat is properly browned, pour in the rest of ingredients in this order: celery, carrots, tomato sauce, tomato paste, red wine, dried chili flakes, and sugar. Mix well.

5. Season with salt and pepper.

6. Stir in the uncooked salad macaroni.

7. Clamp on the lid. Set the pressure cooker on high pressure for 5 minutes, with the normal pressure release option.

8. When the pressure is released, divide the pasta into equal portions. Top off with the freshly grated cheese just before serving. Serve warm.

Recipe #22 : Creamy One Pot Chicken and Vegetable Soup

Preparation Time : 10 minutes
Cooking Time : 10 minutes
Serves:4
Ingredients :

¼ cup cooked chicken breasts or fillets, bones and skins removed, roughly shredded. Leftovers are fine.
You can substitute any boiled or roasted meat, or processed meat like turkey ham. For a meat-free soup, substitute flavored firm tofu instead, cubed.

1cup vegetable broth

½cup mixed frozen vegetables, no need to defrost

½cup heavy cream (You can substitute cashew butter.)

salt, to taste

white pepper, to taste

Directions:

1.Except for the salt and pepper, place all the ingredients of the soup into the pressure cooker pot.

2.Set on low pressure for 10 minutes, with the normal pressure release option.

3. When the pressure is released, carefully remove lid. Ladle out 4 equal portions into serving cups. Serve immediately. You can also store the leftovers in the freezer for later consumption.

Recipe #23 : Easy Mushroom Stew

Preparation Time : 70 minutes, including soaking time
Cooking Time : 20 minutes
Serves:4
Ingredients :

1 piece dried shitake mushroom, washed well under running water, soaked for at least an hour in a cup of water, root and central stem removed, sliced into thin strips, soaking liquid discarded

¼ cup canned straw mushrooms, rinsed well under running water, halved lengthwise, drained well

½ cup fresh button mushrooms, roots trimmed, thinly sliced

1 tsp. extra virgin olive oil

1 piece leek, roots and yellow leaves trimmed, sliced thinly

¼ tsp. garlic powder

¼ tsp. onion powder

dash ginger powder

2 cups vegetable broth

½ cup heavy cream (or to make this a vegan friendly dish, substitute cashew butter) salt, to taste

white pepper, to taste

Garnish

toasted bread or saltines (optional)

Directions:

1.Set the cooker on high pressure. With the lid off, add in the olive oil. Wait for it to become slightly smoky, about 1 minute.

2.Sauté the fresh button mushrooms, until these are somewhat opaque and limp, about 4 minutes.

3.Add in the rest of the ingredients. Season well with salt and pepper. Clamp on the lid. Set the cooker on low pressure, for 15 minutes, with the normal release option.

4.After the pressure is released, the stew is ready to serve. Serve warm with toasted bread or saltines, if desired.

Cooking Tip #8: You can save a lot of money by making fresh spice pastes at home. This is particularly true if you like cooking Asian-inspired dishes. Using a blender or food processor, simply process equal amounts of garlic and ginger to make garlic-ginger paste. If you are not using the paste immediately, store this in an air-tight container, with just enough olive oil to keep the paste slightly submerged. This will keep in the fridge for up to 1 month.

Other spice paste recipes include:

•Garlic, ginger, onion paste – 1 head garlic, 1 thumb-sized ginger, and 2 whole shallots or red onions, plus olive oil.

•Fresh curry paste - 1 head garlic, 1 thumb-sized fresh turmeric, 1 thumb-sized ginger, 2 whole shallots or red onions, 1 piece lemongrass (white part only,) fresh bay leaf, and 1 piece Thai chili (stems removed,) plus olive oil.

Recipe #24 : Spicy Butternut Squash Soup

Preparation Time : 20 minutes
Cooking Time : 14 minutes
Serves:4
Equipment Needed : Blender or food processor
Ingredients :

1Tbsp. extra virgin olive oil

1 piece white onion, large-sized, peeled, roughly chopped

4 cups chicken or vegetable broth

1 pound butternut squash, about 2.2 kilos, peeled, seeded, cubed

½ cup leeks, roots and yellow leaves trimmed off, minced

1 Tbsp. maple syrup. You can use honey or other liquid sweeteners of your choice

¼tsp.India paprika or hot paprika

½tsp. cumin powder

½tsp.cinnamon powder

½ tsp. nutmeg

1 cup heavy cream (or any dairy substitute of your choice)

salt and black pepper, to taste

Directions:

1. Set the cooker on high pressure. Add in the olive oil. Wait until the oil to be slightly smoky, or about 1 minute.

2. Add in the onions. Sauté this until onions become slight opaque, about 3 minutes.

3. Add in the remaining ingredients. Stir. Season with salt and pepper.

4. Clamp on the lid. Set cooker on high pressure for 10 minutes, with the quick release option.

5. When the pressure is released, allow the soup to cool slightly, or about 5 minutes. Carefully ladle out the soup into the blender.

6. Process until smooth. Pour the soup into individual cups. Serve immediately.

Cooking Tip #9: Paprika or powdered red pepper is a very versatile spice. This is a good ingredient to keep in your pantry. It can provide a hint of color to your pressure cooked stews (from deep red to a shade of orange,) and a wonderful hint (or punch) of spiciness. There are many types of powdered paprika (e.g. Delicate, Exquisite Delicate, Rose, Noble Sweet, etc.) but the 2 most common are "Sweet" Paprika (mildest taste, very vibrant color, pungent aroma;) and "Strong" Paprika (fiery hot, dull shade of red, sharp aroma.)

Recipe #25 : Meaty Grain Stew with Spinach

Preparation Time : 25 minutes
Cooking Time : 23 minutes
Serves:4
Ingredients :

¼ pound Italian sausages, casings removed, crumbled into small chunks

1 piece onion, medium-sized, peeled, diced

1 clove garlic, peeled, crushed, minced

¼cupbarley, rinsed well under running water, drained

¼ cup chicken thigh fillet, skin removed, thinly sliced across the grain

4 cups chicken or vegetable broth

½cup canned chickpeas, rinsed well under running water, drained

¼ cuplentils

1 cup frozen spinach

salt, to taste

Directions:

1.Set the cooker on high pressure. With the lid off, brown the crumbled Italian sausage filling. Using a wooden spoon, sauté the meat until most chunks have turned golden, about 5 minutes.

2. Add in the onions and garlic. Continue cooking until these become aromatic, about 3 minutes.
3. Add the rest of the ingredients, except the salt. Gently mix.
4. Clamp on the lid. Set the cooker on high pressure for 15 minutes, with the quick pressure release option.
5. When the pressure is released, let the stew sit undisturbed for 2 minutes. This will allow the barley to absorb more liquid.
6. Taste the stew just before serving. Season with salt, if needed. Serve warm.

Recipe #26 : Chickpea, Potato and Spinach Soup

Preparation Time : 25 minutes
Cooking Time : 19 minutes
Serves:4
Equipment Needed : Blender or food processor
Ingredients :

1 can chickpeas, about 425 grams, rinsed under running water, drained well

2 pieces potatoes, medium-sized, peeled, quartered

1 clove garlic, peeled, crushed, minced

1 piece onion, medium-sized, quartered

1 Tbsp.olive oil

1 cup frozen spinach, no need to thaw

vegetable or chicken broth

salt, to taste

parsley, roughly chopped, for garnish (optional)

croutons or toasted bread, for garnish (optional)

Directions:

1.Set the cooker on high pressure. Add in the olive oil. Wait until the oil becomes slightly smoky, or about 1 minute.

2.Add in the onions and garlic. Sauté until onions become slight opaque, about 3 minutes.

3.Except for the salt, parsley, and the broth, add in the rest of the ingredients. Stir.

4.Pour in just enough vegetable broth to cover the potatoes.

5.Clamp on the lid. Set the cooker on high pressure for 15 minutes, with the quick release option.

6.When cooked, remove the lid. Season with salt, if needed. Let the soup cool down for at least 10 minutes before ladling this into the blender or food processor. Process until smooth.

7.Divide the soup into 4 equal portions. Pour into individual cups.

8.Garnish with chopped parsley, if desired. Serve warm with croutons or toasted bread.

Recipe #27 : Green Soup (Pea and Potato Soup)

Preparation Time : 5 minutes
Cooking Time : 15 minutes
Serves:4
Equipment Needed : food processor or blender
Ingredients :

2 cups frozen peas, no need to thaw

1 cup frozen spinach, no need to thaw

2 pieces potatoes, medium-sized, peeled, cubed

1 tsp. garlic powder

1 tsp.onion powder

vegetable or chicken broth

salt, to taste

white pepper, to taste

 dash Sweet paprika, for garnish (optional)

saltines or crackers, for garnish (optional)

Directions:

1.Except for the vegetable broth, salt, pepper, paprika and saltines, place all the ingredients into the pressure cooker. Stir.
2.Pour in just enough vegetable broth to cover the potatoes.
3.Clamp on the lid. Set the cooker on high pressure for 15 minutes, with the quick release option.

4. When cooked, remove the lid. Season with salt and pepper, if needed. Let the soup cool down for at least 10 minutes before ladling this into the blender or food processor. Process until smooth.

5. Divide the soup into 4 equal portions. Pour into individual cups.

6. Add a dash of sweet paprika per cup for a hint of color. Serve with saltines, if desired.

Recipe #28 : Quick Clam Chowder

Preparation Time : 20 minutes
Cooking Time : 12 minutes
Serves:4
Ingredients :

4 slices pancetta, or any thick sliced bacon of your choice

¼ cup water

1 clove garlic, peeled, minced

1 piece onion, peeled, minced

1 stalk celery, root trimmed, stringy bits removed, minced

1 can whole tomatoes, about 400 ml, roughly chopped

1piece fresh bay leaf

½ piece green bell pepper, cored, deseeded, minced

2 ½ cupsclam juice. You can substitute fish or vegetable broth

1 Tbsp. flour

1 piece potato, large-sized, peeled, minced, soaked in water to prevent browning, drained well just before using

1 cup fresh clams, minced. You can substitute canned clams, but rinse these well under running water to remove most of the pickling salt.

salt, to taste

pepper, to taste

Directions:

1. Set the cooker on high pressure. Tumble in the bacon slices and the quarter cup of water. Clamp on the lid. Set the timer at 2 minutes, with the quick pressure release option. This will immediately render the fat off the bacon.

2. After the pressure has been released, carefully remove the lid. Add in the garlic, onions, and green pepper. Stir.

3. Add in the flour. Stir well. Make sure that the bacon grease has absorbed all of the flour before adding the rest of the ingredients.

4. Tumble in the celery, tomatoes, bay leaf and clam juice.

5. Drain the potatoes and add to the pot.

6. Clamp on the lid and set the timer for 10 minutes, with the normal release option.

7. After the pressure has been released, carefully remove the lid. Stir in the minced clams. Season with salt and pepper. Put the lid back on and let the chowder sit undisturbed for the next 5 to 10 minutes.

8. Just before serving, fish out the bay leaf and discard. Taste the chowder and adjust seasoning, if desired. Serve warm.

Recipe #29 : Easy Onion Soup

Preparation Time : 10 minutes
Cooking Time : 18 minutes
Serves:4
Ingredients :

For the soup

5 pieces white onions, medium-sized, thinly but uniformly sliced to ensure even cooking

2 Tbsp. olive oil

4 cupsvegetable or chicken broth

¼ tsp. freshly ground black pepper

2 Tbsp.dry white wine

¼ tsp. white sugar

salt, to taste

To serve

4 slicestoasted baguette or sour dough bread (optional)

grated Parmesan cheese (optional) To make this dairy or meat free, you can substitute finely chopped parsley

Directions:

1.Set the cooker on high pressure. Add in the oil and the onions at the same time. Give this a stir. Cook until the onions are be quite limp, and a little watery, about 3 minutes.

2.Add in the rest of the soup ingredients. Clamp on the lid. Cook on high pressure for 15 minutes, with the normal release option.

3.After 15 minutes, carefully remove the lid. Taste. Season with salt, if needed.

4.To serve: Ladle the soup into cups. Sprinkle a little Parmesan cheese, if desired. Serve with one slice of toasted bread.

Recipe #30 : Pea Soup in a Flash

Preparation Time : 15 minutes
Cooking Time : 13 minutes
Serves:4
Equipment Needed : Blender or food processor
Ingredients :

1 Tbsp. olive oil

1 piece onion, peeled, minced

4 stems leeks, roots and yellow leaves trimmed, washed, drained well, minced

2 pieces potatoes, peeled, cubed into bite-sized pieces

1 cup frozen peas, no need to thaw

4 cups vegetable or chicken broth

salt, to taste

black pepper, to taste

Directions:

1.Set the cooker on high pressure. Add in the oil and wait until it becomes slightly smoky, about 1 minute.

2.Sauté the onions and leeks until both have softened, about 2 minutes.

3.Except for the salt and pepper, add in all the remaining ingredients. Clamp on the lid, and cook on high pressure for 10 minutes. Choose the quick pressure release option.

4.After cooking, carefully remove the lid. Taste the soup. Season with salt and pepper, if needed. Allow this cool slightly before ladling into the blender or food processor.

5.Process until smooth.

6.Pour in individual cups. Serve immediately.

Recipe #31 : Chunky Tomato Soup with Tortilla Chips

Preparation Time : 10 minutes
Cooking Time : 10 minutes
Serves: 4
Ingredients :

1 clovegarlic, peeled, minced

1 piece onion, peeled, minced

1 piece red bell pepper, halved, cored, deseeded, minced

2 cans tomato chunks

2 cups vegetable or chicken broth

2 Tbsp. sugar

1 tsp. white wine vinegar

½ cup cilantro leaves, roughly chopped, reserve some for garnishing

salt, to taste

black pepper, to taste

To serve

tortilla chips

Directions:

1. Set the cooker on high pressure. Except for the tortilla chips, salt and pepper, add in all the ingredients. Clamp on the lid, and cook on high pressure for 10 minutes. Choose the quick pressure release option.

2. After the pressure has been released, carefully remove the lid. Taste the soup. Season with salt and pepper, if needed.

3. Ladle soup into individual cups. Serve tortilla chips on the side. Serve immediately.

Recipe #32 : Shrimp and Pea Stew

Preparation Time : 2 minutes
Cooking Time : 10 minutes
Serves:4
Ingredients :

1 cup frozen shrimps, no need to thaw

1 cup frozen peas, no need to thaw

4 cups fish or vegetable broth

¼ tsp. fish sauce

black pepper, to taste

To serve

1 piecelemon or lime, cut into wedges

drops roasted sesame oil. Plain sesame oil works with this recipe as well. If you do not have peanut allergy, you can also substitute peanut oil. (optional)

cilantro leaves, roughly chopped, for garnish

Directions:

1.Place frozen shrimps, peas and fish broth into the pressure cooker. Clamp on the lid and let this cook on high pressure for 10 minutes. Choose the quick release option.

2.Once the pressure has been released, carefully remove the lid. Season the soup with fish sauce and pepper, if needed.

3. To serve: ladle soup into individual cups. Add one drop of roasted sesame oil into each cup. (Do not add more, or the sesame oil will overpower the taste of the soup.)

4. Garnish with a sprinkling of cilantro leaves.

5. Just before serving, squeeze a few drops of lemon juice into the soup. Serve warm.

Recipe #33 : Squash Soup

Preparation Time : 20 minutes
Cooking Time : 10 minutes
Serves:4
Equipment Needed : blender or food processor
Ingredients :

1 whole butternut squash, medium-sized, peeled, deseeded, cubed

1 piece carrot, medium-sized, ends removed, unpeeled, cubed

1 stalk leek, roots and yellow leaves removed, roughly chopped

1 handful fresh parsley, roots and yellow leaves removed, roughly chopped

4 cups vegetable or chicken broth

salt, to taste

black pepper, to taste

To serve

cilantro leaves, roughly chopped, for garnish

 splash cream, milk, or half-and-half. You can substitute cashew butter, for a vegan-friendly dish

Directions:

1.Except for the cilantro leaves, cream, salt and pepper, place all of the soup ingredients into the pressure cooker. Set the cooker on high pressure for 10 minutes, with the quick pressure release option.

2. Once the pressure has been released, carefully remove the lid. Season soup with salt and pepper.

3. Let the soup cool for at least 1 minute before ladling into the blender or food processor. Process until the soup looks smooth and creamy.

4. To serve: ladle soup into individual cups. Garnish with a sprinkling of cilantro leaves and a splash of cream. Serve warm.

Recipe #34 : Cold Yogurt Soup with Barley and Mint
Preparation Time : 25 minutes (including the chill time)
Cooking Time : 20 minutes
Serves:4
Equipment Needed : blender or food processor
Ingredients :

2 Tbsp. extra virgin olive oil

1 piece onion, peeled, minced

3 Tbsp. pearl barley, rinsed, drained well (You can substitute quinoa, to make this dish gluten-free.)

4 cups vegetable or chicken broth

2 cups plain or unflavored yogurt

salt, to taste

pepper, to taste

fresh mint, washed, pat dried, minced, for garnish

bread or cracker, for garnish (optional)

Directions:

1.Set the cooker on high pressure. Add in the oil and heat until slightly smoky, about 1 minute.

2.Sauté the onions in the hot oil, until these turn limp and slightly opaque, about 3 minutes.

3.Add in the pearl barley and vegetable broth. Gently stir. Clamp on the lid. Set on high pressure for 15 minutes, and choose the normal pressure release option.

4.Once the pressure is released, carefully remove the lid. Ladle the soup into a heat-resistant, freezer-safe container. Place in the freezer for 15 minutes, to quickly bring down its temperature.

5.When the soup is well-chilled, stir in the yogurt. Season well with salt and pepper. Divide the soup into 4 equal portions. Just before serving, garnish with a sprinkling of fresh mint. Serve cold with bread or crackers.

Recipe #35 : 10 Vegetables in a Soup

Preparation Time : 30 minutes
Cooking Time : 19 minutes
Serves:4
Ingredients :

1 head cauliflower, washed, drained, cut into florets

1 headbroccoli, washed, drained, cut into florets

1 piece carrot, top removed, unpeeled, cubed

1 piece potato, peeled, cubed

1 piece sweet potato, peeled, cubed

1 piece parsnip, peeled, cubed

1 piece celeriac, peeled, cubed

2 cups squash, peeled, cubed

½ head cabbage, washed well, drained, center core removed, quartered

4 leaves napa cabbage, washed well, lower ends trimmed, sliced thickly into long strips

1 piece onion, peeled, minced

1 clove garlic, peeled, minced

2 pieces tomatoes, washed, halved, seeds removed, minced

1 tsp. extra virgin olive oil

1 tsp. Spanish or sweet paprika

1 piece habanero or Thai chili, top removed, halved, seeds removed, minced

2 cups vegetable broth

salt and pepper, to taste

For garnish

fresh chives, washed, pat dried, roots and yellow leaves removed, minced

Note: to ensure even cooking, make sure that the vegetables are cut in approximately the same sizes, preferably, into bite-sized pieces. At the very least, try to cube the vegetables to the same size as the broccoli and cauliflower florets.

Adjust also the volume of your vegetables, in case you are working with a small pressure cooker.

Directions:

1.Set the cooker on high pressure. Add in the oil and heat until slightly smoky, about 1 minute.

2.Sauté the onions and garlic in the hot oil, until the onions turn limp and slightly opaque, about 3 minutes. Stir constantly to prevent the garlic from burning.

3.Stir in the tomatoes and habanero.

4.Add the vegetable broth.

5.Very carefully, tumble in the rest of the ingredients, except for the cabbage and the napa cabbage. Stir.

6.Clamp on the lid. Set on high pressure for 15 minutes, and choose the normal pressure release option.

7.Once the pressure is released, lift up the lid and add in the cabbages and napa cabbages. Close the lid, and let the soup sit undisturbed for 10 more minutes. This allows the cabbages to cook, but still retain their crispiness.

8.After 5 minutes, remove the lid of the cooker. Season the soup with salt and pepper, if needed.

9.Ladle the thick soup into 4 separate bowls. Garnish with minced chives. Serve immediately.

Recipe #36 : No Fuss Chicken Soup

Preparation Time : 10 minutes
Cooking Time : 20 minutes
Serves:4
Ingredients :

½ pound chicken thigh fillets, washed, pat dried with paper towels, skins removed, diced

¼ tsp. garlic powder

¼tsp. onion powder

¼ tsp. Spanish paprika

1 piece leek, root and yellow leaves removed, sliced into thin, diagonal strips, reserve a pinch, for garnish

4 cups chicken broth or vegetable broth

salt, to taste

black pepper, to taste

fresh bread, for garnish (optional)

Directions:

1.Except for the saltines, salt and pepper, place all the ingredients into the pressure cooker pot.

2.Clamp on the lid. Set on high pressure for 15 minutes, and choose the normal pressure release option.

3.Once the pressure is released, season the soup with salt and pepper, if needed.

4.Ladle the soup into 4 separate bowls. Garnish with the reserved leek slices. Serve warm with fresh bread.

Recipe #37 : Sour Shrimp with Daikon and Water Spinach

Preparation Time : 15 minutes
Cooking Time : 15 minutes
Serves:4
Ingredients :

½ pound tiger prawns, shells on, approximately 2 to 3 pieces of prawns per person

1 pieceonion, peeled, quartered

4 pieces tomatoes, quartered

1 piece daikon or Japanese radish, ends removed, peeled, cubed into bite-sized pieces

¼ pound water Spinach, also called Chinese spinach, leaves and tender shoots only, washed and drained well

1 tsp. whole peppercorns

1 tsp. good quality fish sauce, add more, if needed

1 Tbsp. tamarind paste (or ½ Tbsp. tamarind concentrate) add more, if desired

cooked rice (optional)

Directions:

1.Except for the rice, water spinach and the tiger prawns, add all the ingredients into the pressure cooker pot.

2.Clamp on the lid. Set on high pressure for 10 minutes, and choose the quick pressure release option.

3.Once the pressure is released, add in the tiger prawns and the water spinach. Clamp on the lid once more, and set on high pressure for 5 minutes. Choose the normal release option, this time.

4.When the pressure is released, carefully remove the lid. Taste the broth. Adjust the seasonings according to taste.

5.You can serve this as is, or with a bowl of warm rice. Serve immediately.

Recipe #38 : Sour Pork with Daikon and Taro

Preparation Time : 20 minutes
Cooking Time : 25 minutes
Serves:4
Ingredients :

½ pound pork belly, skins removed, cubed, washed, pat dried

1 piece taro, large-sized, peeled, cubed

1 pieceonion, peeled, quartered

4 pieces tomatoes, quartered

1 piece daikon or Japanese radish, ends removed, peeled, cubed approximately the size of the pork belly

¼ pound water Spinach, also called Chinese spinach, leaves and tender shoots only, washed and drained well

1 tsp. whole peppercorns

2 tsp. good quality fish sauce, add more, if needed

1 Tbsp. tamarind paste (or ½ Tbsp. tamarind concentrate) add more, if desired

Directions:

1.Except for the water spinach (which cooks almost instantly,) add all the ingredients into the pressure cooker pot.

2.Clamp on the lid. Set on high pressure for 25 minutes. Choose the quick pressure release option.

3.Once the pressure is released, add in the water spinach. Close the lid, and let the stew sit undisturbed for the next 10 minutes. This will allow the water spinach to cook, but still remain crisp.

4.After 10 minutes, stir the soup. Using a fork, mash the cooked taro a little. This will thicken the broth a little.

5.Taste the broth. Adjust seasonings according to taste. Serve warm.

Recipe #39 : Vegetable Curry in Lemongrass Coconut Sauce

Preparation Time : 30 minutes
Cooking Time : 16 minutes
Serves:4
Equipment Needed : food processor; rubber spatula
Ingredients :

For the flavor base

2 Tbsp. extra virgin olive oil

1 piece onion, peeled, roughly chopped

3 cloves garlic, peeled, crushed

1 piece ginger, thumb-sized, peeled, roughly chopped

2 pieces lemongrass, white parts only, root removed, bulbs bruised using the flat of the knife, roughly chopped

1 piece habanero or Thai chili, top removed, halved, seeds removed, minced

The vegetables

1 head cauliflower, washed, drained, cut into small florets

1 piece carrot, top removed, unpeeled, diced

2 pieces potatoes, peeled, diced

1 piece sweet potato, peeled, diced

1 piece bell pepper, cored, deseeded, diced

1 piece squash, small-sized, peeled, deseeded, diced

For the seasonings

¼ tsp. strong or spicy paprika (also sometimes called Indian paprika) You can substitute powdered cayenne pepper

¼ tsp. turmeric powder

¼ tsp. all spice powder. You can substitute 5 spice powder in a pinch.

1 tsp. garam masala of your choice

dash black pepper powder

dash coriander seeds powder

dash cumin seeds powder

1 tsp. brown sugar

1 tsp. good quality fish sauce

2 cups vegetable broth

2 cans coconut milk, divided

salt, to taste

As side dish warm pita or naan bread (optional)

Directions:

1. Place all the ingredients of the flavor base into a food processor. Process until everything has turned into a smooth paste. You can do this beforehand. See Cooking Tip#8 on page 62.

2. Set the cooker on high pressure. Using a rubber spatula, scrape the paste into the cooker. Sauté this for at least 1 minute, stirring constantly.

3. Except for the salt, the vegetable broth and the coconut milk, add in all the seasonings, still stirring constantly.

4. Add in all the vegetables, then the broth and one can of coconut milk. Clamp on the lid, and set the cooker on high pressure for 15 minutes, with the normal pressure release option.

5. After the pressure has been released, stir in the remaining can of coconut milk. Clamp on the lid once more, and let the curry sit undisturbed for at least 5 minutes.

6. After 5 minutes, give the curry a stir. Taste. Add salt, only if needed. Ladle into individual cups. Serve with warm pita or naan bread.

Recipe #40 : Spicy Italian Sausage Stew

Preparation Time : 10 minutes
Cooking Time : 12 minutes
Serves:4
Ingredients :

2 links fresh or smoked Italian sausages, cubed

2 pieces onions, peeled, roughly chopped

1 piecered bell pepper, cored, deseeded, cubed

1 Tbsp.chili flakes

1 piece Thai chili, top removed, minced

1 Tbsp. Spanish paprika

1 Tbsp.white wine vinegar

2cups beef or chicken broth

salt, to taste

pepper, to taste

As side dish1 slice of bread per person (optional) or ...
bed of pasta, approximately ½ cup per person
(optional)

Directions:

1.Set the cooker on high pressure. Place in the sausages and the white wine vinegar. Simmer for 1 minute, or until the fat renders from the sausages. Stir constantly to prevent the meat from sticking to the bottom of the pot.

2. Add in the onions and bell peppers, and cook for a further 1 minute.

3. Add in the chicken broth, the Spanish paprika, the Thai chili, and the chili flakes. Clamp on the lid. Set the cooker on high pressure for 10 minutes with the normal pressure release option.

4. Once the pressure is released, carefully remove the lid. Divide the stew into 4 equal portions. Ladle into individual plates. This could be served plain, or with a slice of bread, or on a bed of cooked pasta. This is also a great dish served chilled.

Recipe #41 : Meaty Beef Broth

Preparation Time : 20 minutes
Cooking Time : 30 minutes
Serves:4
Ingredients :

½pound bone-in beef shanks, visible fats trimmed off

1 piece whole onion, peeled, halved

1 stem celery, lower end trimmed, sliced into 4 long slivers

1 piece carrot, top and lower end removed, unpeeled, sliced into 4 large chunks

1 piece parsnip, top and lower end removed, peeled, halved

3 cups vegetable broth, or plain water

salt, to taste

white pepper, to taste

Directions:

1.Except for the salt and pepper, place all the ingredients into the pressure cooker.

2.Set the cooker on high pressure for 30 minutes, with the natural pressure release option.

3.When the pressure is released, taste to see if the broth needs further seasoning. Add salt and pepper, only if needed.

Note: this broth can be served as a light meal. Or, it could be used as flavor base for other dishes.

If you are using it as a flavor base:

• Let the broth cool completely at room temperature first.

• Place the broth inside the freezer for at least 30 minutes. The rendered fat will solidify on top. Scoop out the excess fat and discard.

• Take the cooked shank, and discard the bone. Shred and chop the meat and set aside. The cooked meat can be used for other recipes. See Recipe # ???

• Using a blender or food processor, puree the broth including the vegetables.

• Run the processed broth through a sieve to remove the larger chunks of vegetables. Discard the latter.

• Store the broth in an air-tight, freezer-safe container. Keep this in the deep freeze, until needed.

Recipe #42 : Meaty Pork Broth

Preparation Time : 20 minutes
Cooking Time : 20 minutes
Serves:4
Ingredients :

½pound ham hock or pork knuckles, visible fats trimmed off

1 piece whole onion, peeled

1 piece carrot, top and lower end removed, unpeeled, sliced into 4 large chunks

1 piece potato, peeled, quartered

1 piece sweet potato, peeled, quartered

3 cups vegetable broth, or plain water

salt, to taste

white pepper, to taste

Directions:

1. Except for the salt and pepper, place all the ingredients into the pressure cooker.

2. Set the cooker on high pressure for 20 minutes, with the natural pressure release option.

3. When the pressure is released, taste to see if the broth needs further seasoning. Add salt and pepper, only if needed.

Note: this broth can be served as a light meal. Serve warm with bread or saltines.
It could be used as flavor base for other dishes.

If you are using it as a flavor base:

- Let the broth cool completely at room temperature first.

- Place the broth inside the freezer for at least 30 minutes. The rendered fat will solidify on top. Scoop out the excess fat and discard.

- Take the cooked ham hock, and discard the skin and bone. Shred and chop the meat and set aside. The cooked meat can be used for other recipes. See Recipe #46: Quick, Easy, Chewy Miso Soup on page 95.

- Using a blender or food processor, puree the broth including the vegetables. The broth would look thick and gooey, due to the collagen in the ham hock.

- Store the broth in an air-tight, freezer-safe container. Keep this in the deep freeze, until needed.

Recipe #43 : Meaty Chicken Broth

Preparation Time : 20 minutes
Cooking Time : 20 minutes
Serves:4
Ingredients :

½ pound bone-in, skin-on chicken thighs

1 piece whole onion, peeled

1 piece carrot, top and lower end removed, unpeeled, sliced into 4 large chunks

2 stems leeks, roots and yellow leaves removed, roughly chopped

2 tbsp. fresh cilantro, roughly chopped

1 piece fresh oregano leaf, washed well, roughly shredded (You can substitute ½ tsp. oregano powder.

3 cups vegetable broth, or plain water

salt, to taste

white pepper, to taste

Directions:

1. Except for the salt and pepper, place all the ingredients into the pressure cooker.

2. Set the cooker on high pressure for 20 minutes, with the natural pressure release option.

3. When the pressure is released, taste to see if the broth needs further seasoning. Add salt and pepper, only if needed.

Note: this broth can be served as a light meal. Serve warm with bread.
It could be used as flavor base for other dishes.

If you are using it as a flavor base:

- Let the broth cool completely at room temperature first.

- Place the broth inside the freezer for at least 30 minutes. The rendered fat will solidify on top. Scoop out the excess fat and discard.

- Take the cooked chicken thighs, and discard skins and bones. Shred and chop the meat and set aside. The cooked meat can be used for other recipes. See Recipe #22: Creamy One Pot Chicken and Vegetable Soup on page 66.

• Run the processed broth through a sieve to remove large chunks of vegetables. Discard the latter.

• Store the broth in an air-tight, freezer-safe container. Keep this in the deep freeze, until needed.

Recipe #44 : Easy Fish Broth With Herbs

Preparation Time : 20 minutes
Cooking Time : 15 minutes
Serves:4
Equipment Needed :pastry brush
Ingredients :

4pieces fish fillets, preferably thick-cut with low fat content, e.g. black or red grouper, amberjack, catfish, mahi-mahi, snapper or tilefish

Note: the thicker the fillet cut, the better. This will prevent the fish from breaking apart while cooking.

If you would rather not have fish, you can always substitute shrimps or prawns. If you would rather have shellfish, always choose fresh, live shellfish (not canned or frozen.) Clams work well with this recipe, but you can also try mussels.

2 stems leeks, roots and yellow leaves removed, roughly chopped

1 tsp. fresh parsley, roughly chopped

1 tsp. fresh rosemary, roughly chopped

3 cups vegetable broth, or plain water

1 piece lemon, juiced, seeds removed, divided

extra virgin olive oil, for greasing

good quality fish sauce, to taste

white pepper, to taste

Directions:

1. Using a pastry brush and the olive oil, lightly grease the cooking surface's bottom and sides.

2. Carefully place all four fish fillets on the cooking surface. Take care not to overlap the fillets, or these will stick together during cooking.

If you are using a small pressure cooker, either cook this recipe in 2 batches (using half portions,) or you can trim your fish fillets so they can fit into the pot.

3. Except for the lemon juice, fish sauce and pepper, place all the ingredients into the pressure cooker.

4. Set the cooker on low pressure for 15 minutes, with the natural pressure release option.

5. When the pressure is released, taste to see if the broth needs further seasoning. Add fish sauce and pepper, only if needed.

6. Very carefully scoop out each fish fillet and place on individual plates. Divide the lemon juice into 4 equal portions. Sprinkle each portion on top of the fish fillets. Serve immediately.

Note: this broth can be served as a light meal, or it could be used as flavor base for other dishes.

If you are using it as a flavor base:

- Let the broth cool completely at room temperature first.

- Carefully lift out the fish fillets. Using a fork, flake the meat and set aside. The cooked meat can be used for other recipes. See Recipe #???.

- Using a food processor, puree the broth. Run the liquid through a sieve to remove large chunks of herbs. Discard the latter.

- Store the broth in an air-tight, freezer-safe container. Keep this in the deep freeze, until needed. The fish broth will only keep fresh in the freezer for 1 week.

Recipe #45 : Grouper in Ginger Soup with Cabbage

Preparation Time : 20 minutes
Cooking Time : 15 minutes
Serves:4
Ingredients :

½ poundred or black grouper fillets. You can substitute amberjack, mahi-mahi, or snapper

4 pieces shallots, peeled, quartered

1 piece ginger, thumb-sized, peeled, grated

2 stems leeks, roots and yellow leaves removed, minced, reserve some, for garnish

½ head white cabbage, cored, quartered

3 cupsvegetable broth or plain water

1 piece fresh bay leaf

1 tsp. whole peppercorns

good quality fish sauce, to taste

Directions:

1. Except for the fish sauce, place all the ingredients into the pressure cooker.

2. Set the cooker on low pressure, for 15 minutes, with the normal pressure release option.

3. When the pressure is released, taste the fish broth to see if it needs further seasoning. Add the fish sauce, only when needed.

4. Serve warm.

Recipe #46 : Quick, Easy, Chewy Miso Soup
Preparation Time : 30 minutes
Cooking Time : 13 minutes

Serves: 4
Ingredients :

For the ramen soup base

2 cloves garlic, peeled, minced

1 piece ginger, thumb-sized, peeled, grated

1 piece shallot, peeled, minced

1 Tbsp. sesame oil

¼ pound cooked pork, sliced thinly, or shredded (See notes on page 88, under Recipe #42: Meaty Pork Broth.)

¼ pound cooked beef, sliced thinly, or shredded (See notes on page 86, under Recipe #41: Meaty Beef Broth.)

1 tsp. chili bean sauce. You can substitute hoisin sauce.

4 Tbsp. awase miso or any mild-tasting miso paste

1 Tbsp. mirin or Japanese sake. You can substitute rice wine, or any mild-flavored cooking wine.

1 Tbsp. sugar

4 cups chicken broth

1 tsp. salt

white pepper, to taste

For the noodles

4 servingsfresh or dried ramen noodles, about 1 cup each serving, cooked according to package instructions. Drain well. Divide into 4 equal parts. Add ½ tsp. oil per serving to prevent the noodles from sticking together.
In a pinch, you can also substitute instant ramen noodles. Discard the soup packages. Do not cook. The noodles will cook when the hot broth is poured over it. Serving the noodles immediately will give you that chewy texture.

For the toppings

¼ pound cooked ham, or any mild-flavored kind of ham, sliced thinly, divided into 4 equal portions

2 pieces soft boiled eggs, halved, One portion = ½ egg

1 cup bean sprouts, washed well, lightly blanched, divided into 4 equal portions

1/2 cup canned whole corn kernels, rinsed well under running water, drained, divided into 4 equal portions

4 pieces roasted nori sheets, cut into 3 x 3 inch squares

2 stalksleeks, root and yellow leaves, removed, washed well, minced or julienned, divided into 4 equal portions

dropschili oil (optional)

drops roasted sesame oil (optional)

drops light soy sauce, or sushi soy sauce (optional)

Directions:

1. Set the cooker on high pressure. Heat the sesame oil for the ramen soup base until slightly smoky, about 1 minute.
2. Sauté the garlic, ginger and shallots until aromatic, about 2 minutes.
3. Add in the rest of the ingredients for the ramen soup base. Stir.
4. Clamp on the lid. Set the timer for 10 minutes with the quick pressure release option.
5. To serve: prepare 4 deep ramen bowls (or large soup cups.) Place one portion of the noodles per bowl.
6. Artfully arrange the cooked ham, soft boiled eggs, blanched bean sprouts, corn kernels, roasted nori sheets, and leeks on top of the noodles.
7. Once the pressure is released, remove the lid of the cooker. Carefully, ladle the soup into the prepared ramen bowls in equal portions.
8. If using, place a few drops of chili oil, roasted sesame oil, and light soy sauce. Serve immediately.

Recipe #47 : Spicy Beef Sandwich

Preparation Time : 10 minutes
Cooking Time : 10 minutes
Serves:4
Ingredients :

For the sandwich filling

4 cups boiled beef shanks, shredded and minced. You can substitute any cooked beef item such as corned beef or pastrami (See notes on page 86 under Recipe #41:

Meaty Beef Broth.)

1 cup beef or vegetable broth

1 stem leek, root and yellow leaves removed, minced

1 piece bell pepper, cored, deseeded, minced

For the sandwich

4 pieces split Kaiser rolls, or sourdough rolls. You can substitute any dense, mild tasting bread. In a pinch, you can use hamburger buns toasted on the insides.

1 piece Thai chili, minced, mixed with ...

4 Tbsp. plain mayonnaise, or any mayo substitute of your choice

4 tsp. English mustard

4 slices Swiss cheese, or any semi-hard cheese of your choice, e.g. Provolone, Beaufort or gruyere

Directions:

1. Place all the ingredients of the sandwich filling into the pressure cooker pot. Clam on the lid.

2. Set the cooker on low pressure, for 10 minutes with the normal pressure release option.

3. To assemble the sandwich: spread the mustard on the top half of the Kaiser rolls; and the chili-mayo mix on the bottom half.

4. Place a slice of cheese on top of the chili-mayo mix.

5. Once the pressure is released, carefully spoon out equal portions of the cooked beef into the prepared sandwiches, including some of its cooking liquid. Serve immediately.

Recipe #48 : Pulled Pork Sandwich in a Pot

Preparation Time : 20 minutes
Cooking Time : 10 minutes
Serves:4
Equipment Needed : sieve or strainer; microwave
Ingredients :

For the sandwich filling

4 cups cooked ham hocks or pork knuckles, skins and bones removed, shredded and minced. You can substitute any cooked pork item e.g. leftover pork roast. (See notes on page 88 under Recipe #42: Meaty Pork Broth.)

You can also substitute cooked chicken for this recipe. (See notes on page 91 under Recipe #43: Meaty Chicken Broth.)

2 cups brown sugar, packed

1 Tbsp. good quality maple syrup

1 Tbsp. honey

2 Tbsp. garlic powder

2 Tbsp. onion powder

2 Tbsp. ground white pepper

2 Tbsp. Spanish paprika

2 Tbsp. dried red pepper flakes

1 cup pork or vegetable broth

½ cup hot sauce

pinch sea salt or kosher salt

For the barbecue sauce

4 cups catsup

1 cup honey

1 clove garlic, peeled, grated

2 Tbsp. hot pepper sauce

dash black pepper

pinch sea salt or kosher salt

For the sandwich

4 pieces split Kaiser rolls, or sourdough rolls. You can substitute any dense, mild tasting bread. In a pinch, you can use hamburger buns toasted on the insides.

2 cups homemade or store-bought coleslaw, well-chilled, divide into 4 equal portions

4 pieces whole pickles, drained well (optional)

Directions:

1. Place all the sandwich filling ingredients in the pressure cooker. Set on low pressure for 10 minutes with the normal pressure release option.

2. In a microwave-safe bowl, combine all the ingredients of the barbecue sauce. Mix well. Microwave on high for 30 seconds. Mix again. Set aside.

3. When the pressure is released, carefully ladle the cooked pork into a sieve. Strain out most of the cooking liquid. Discard liquid.

4. Mix the shredded pork with the barbecue sauce. Divide into 4 equal portions.

5. To assemble: take a Kaiser roll. Spread one portion of the shredded pork, and spread on the bottom half of the bread.

6. Place one portion of coleslaw on top of the pulled pork. Top off with the top half of the Kaiser roll. Serve with a pickle (if using) on the side. Serve immediately.

Recipe #49 : Fresh Tuna Salad Sandwich with Lemon Mayo

Preparation Time : 20 minutes
Cooking Time : 5 minutes
Serves:4
Equipment Needed : sieve or strainer, fork, rubber spatula
Ingredients :

For the tuna filling

½ pound fresh albacore tuna fillets, thick-cuts

1 cup water

1 tsp. good quality fish sauce

1 tsp. red chili flakes

For the salad

1 cup mayonnaise, or any mayo substitute of your choice

1 tsp. freshly grated lemon zest

1 Tbsp. lemon juice

1 piece sweet onion, peeled, minced

1 stalk celery, bottom end trimmed, minced

¼ cup raisins

1 Tbsp. pickle relish

1 tbsp. sugar

pinch dill fronds, minced

pinch chives, minced

salt, to taste

white pepper, to taste

For the sandwich

4 pieces split Kaiser rolls, or sourdough rolls. You can substitute any dense, mild tasting bread. In a pinch, you can use hamburger buns toasted on the insides.

4 pieces butterhead or romaine lettuce, large-sized, trimmed, washed, pat dried

8 slices fresh cucumber, skins on

 dashSpanish paprika

Directions:

1.Place all the ingredients of the tuna filling into the pressure cooker. Set on high pressure for 5 minutes with the quick pressure release option.

2.When the pressure is released, carefully ladle the cooked fish into a sieve. Strain out most of the cooking liquid. Discard liquid.

3. Place the cooked tuna in a large bowl. Using a fork, flake the meat. Place the bowl in the freezer for at least 10 minutes to quickly bring down its temperature.

4. To make the salad: in a small bowl, combine lemon juice and sugar. Mix well until the sugar is fully dissolved.

5. Take out the now chilled tuna from the freezer.

6. Pour in the lemon juice-sugar mixture, along with the rest of the ingredients for the salad. Using a rubber spatula, gently fold the mixture until most of the tuna flakes are coated with mayonnaise.

7. Season well with salt and pepper.

8. Divide the tuna salad into 4 equal portions.

9. To assemble: place 2 slices of cucumber each on the bottom halves of the Kaiser bread.

10. Place one portion of tuna salad on top of the cucumbers. Place a dash of Spanish paprika on top of the salad.

11. Place one lettuce leaf, fold side down, on each tuna salad.

12. Top off with the other half of the bread. Serve immediately.

Recipe #50 : Chicken Liver with Spicy Herbed Rice

Preparation Time : 30 minutes
Cooking Time : 12 minutes
Serves: 4

Equipment Needed : spice grinder or food processor

Ingredients :

For the tuna filling

1 Tbsp. extra virgin olive oil

1 piece onion, large-sized, peeled, roughly chopped

250 grams chicken livers, washed well, pat dried, cubed

1 link fresh Italian sausage, or any fresh sausage of your choice, casing removed, roughly chopped

2 stalks celery, bottom end trimmed, minced

2 pieces garlic cloves, peeled, grated

2 cups Basmati rice or any long grain rice

2 ½ cups vegetable stock or plain water

handful fresh parsley, for garnish (optional)

Tabasco sauce (optional)

For the herbs

½ tsp. paprika powder

¼ tsp. cayenne pepper powder

½ tsp. oregano powder

½ tsp. thyme powder

¼ tsp. cumin powder

¼ tsp. salt

¼ tsp. black pepper powder

Directions:

1. Place all the herbs into a spice grinder or food processor. Process until these have turned into fine powder. Set aside.

2. Set the cooker on high pressure. Heat the oil until slightly smoky, about 1 minute. Add in the onions and garlic. Cook until onions turn limp, about 2 minutes.

3. Add in the chopped chicken livers. Sauté until the meat turns slightly brown, about 5 minutes.

4. Stir in the sausages and the celery. Cook for another minute.

5. Add in the rest of the ingredients, along with the powdered herbs. Stir while scraping the bottom of the pan.

6. Clamp on the lid. Set the cooker on high pressure for 5 minutes, with the normal pressure release option.

7. After the pressure is released, let the rice sit undisturbed for the next 5 to 10 minutes. This will allow the chicken livers to absorb more liquid.

8. Divide the rice into 4 equal portions. Serve each portion on a plate.

9. Top off with a sprinkling of fresh parsley and a dash of Tabasco sauce, if desired. Serve warm.

Chapter 8: Delicious Pressure Cooker Dinner Recipes

Recipe #51 : Beef Stew with Parsnips

Preparation Time : 20 minutes
Cooking Time : 9 to 13 minutes – sautéing and browning; 30 minutes
Serves:4
Ingredients :

1 pound beef chuck or top chuck, cubed. You can substitute other lean cuts like rump roast, top round, or round tip roast. You can also substitute lean meat like venison, goat and lamb.

2 Tbsp. extra virgin olive oil

1 piece onion, peeled, minced

1 clove garlic, peeled, minced

1 piece carrot, ends removed, unpeeled, cubed roughly the size of the beef cubes

1 piece potato, peeled, cubed roughly thesize of the beef cubes

1 piece sweet potato, peeled, cubed roughly the size of the beef cubes

1 piece parsnips, peeled, cubed roughly the size of the beef

cubes

½ cup frozen peas, no need to thaw

½ cup tomato sauce

½ cup good quality red wine. This does not have to be the expensive kind, just the type of wine you can drink at the table.

1 sprig fresh thyme, whole, washed and pat dried. You can substitute 1 Tbsp. dried thyme, or 1 tsp. thyme powder.

1 tsp. Worcestershire sauce

½ cupwater, add more, if needed

salt and black pepper, to taste

Directions:

1. Set the cooker on high pressure. Add in the olive oil, and wait until it becomes smoky, about 1 minute.

2. Tumble in the meat, and brown well on all sides. This should take about 2 minutes per side.

3. Except for the salt and pepper, add the rest of the ingredients into the pot. Make sure that most of the meat is covered with water. Add more, if needed.

4. Clamp on the lid. Set the cooker on high pressure for 30 minutes, with the normal pressure release option.

5. Once cooked, season well with salt and pepper. Serve warm.

Recipe #52 : Beef Stew with Peanut Sauce and Vegetables

Preparation Time : 30 minutes
Cooking Time : 30 minutes
Serves:4
Ingredients :

For the stew

¼ pound ox tripe, cleaned well, visible fat trimmed, cubed into bite-sized pieces (You can ask your butcher to do this for you at the store.)

¼ pound ox tail, cleaned well, sliced thickly (You can ask your butcher to do this for you at the store.)

Note: if you would rather not use ox tripe or ox tail, other beef cuts you can use in this recipe are: shoulder top blade, chuck steak, chuck eye steak, ranch steak, shoulder steak and chuck roast. Cube the meat into bite-sized pieces.

1 tsp. garlic powder

1 tsp. onion powder

1 Tbsp. good quality fish sauce, add more later, if desired

1 tsp. whole peppercorns

3 cups water

The vegetables

1 head cabbage, cored, quartered

1 head bok choy or Chines cabbage, lower end removed, individual stems washed, drained well, sliced into 3 inch long slivers

2 pieces okra, ends removed, halved

4 to 6 stems Chinese spinach, individual stems washed, drained well, use only the leaves and the tender stems, discard the rest, yield about ½ cup

For the peanut sauce

½ cup chunky peanut butter, dissolved in…

1 cup boiling water

For serving

steamed or boiled rice

Directions:

1. Place all the ingredients of the stew into the pressure cooker. Set the cooker on high pressure for 20 minutes, with the normal pressure release option.

2. After the pressure is released, stir in the peanut sauce.

3. Add in all the vegetables.

4. Set the cooker again on high pressure for 10 minutes, with the normal pressure release option.

5. After the pressure is released, taste the broth. Add more fish sauce, if needed.

6. Serve warm with rice.

Recipe #53 : Beef Stew with Tomato-Peanut Sauce

Preparation Time : 30 minutes
Cooking Time : 30 minutes
Serves:4
Ingredients :

For the stew

½ poundchuck eye steak, but you can also substitute ranch steak or flat iron steak. Cube the meat into bite-sized pieces.

1 tsp. garlic powder

1 tsp. onion powder

1 piece garlic clove, peeled, crushed

1 piece onion, peeled, halved

1 piece ginger, thumb-sized, peeled, crushed

1 piece dried bay leaf, whole

3 pieces tomatoes, medium-sized, halved, deseeded

1 Tbsp. good quality fish sauce, add more later, if desired

1 tsp. whole peppercorns

3 cups water

For the tomato-peanut sauce

½ cup chunky peanut butter, dissolved in…

1 cup boiling water

½ cup tomato paste

For serving

steamed or boiled rice

Directions:

1. Place all the ingredients of the stew into the pressure cooker. Set the cooker on high pressure for 20 minutes, with the normal pressure release option.

2. After the pressure is released, stir in the tomato-peanut sauce.

3. Set the cooker again on high pressure for 10 minutes, with the normal pressure release option.

4. After the pressure is released, taste the broth. Add more fish sauce, if needed.

5. Serve warm with rice.

Recipe #53 : Seafood Laksa

Preparation Time : 30 minutes
Cooking Time : 27 minutes
Serves:4
Equipment Needed : food processor
Ingredients :

For the spice mix

1 piece lemongrass, root and leaves trimmed, use only the white part, roughly chopped

2 pieces garlic cloves, peeled

1 pieceshallot or red onion, peeled, quartered

1 piece fresh turmeric, thumb-sized, peeled, quartered. You can substitute ginger, or about ½ tsp. turmeric powder.

1 stem leek, root and yellow leaves trimmed, roughly chopped

1 piece Thai chili, stem removed, halved

2 Tbsp. extra virgin olive oil

Seafood Ingredients

4 pieces fish fillets, preferably thick-cut with low fat content, e.g. black or red grouper, snapper or amberjack

4 pieces tiger prawns, shell on, heads removed, about 1 prawn per person. You can use smaller shrimps, about 4 to 5 shrimps per person.

¼ pound squid, skins removed, cleaned well, sliced into thick rings (You can ask your fishmonger to do this for you.) You can also substitute frozen squid rings, but make sure you thaw these out completely in the fridge before using.

For the flavor base

1 Tbsp. good quality fish sauce

1 tsp. Spanish or sweet paprika

¼ tsp. black pepper

1 cup fish or vegetable broth, or plain water

2 cans coconut milk, divided

Directions:

1. Except for the olive oil, process all the ingredients of the spice mix using a food processor.

2. Set the cooker on high pressure. Pour in the olive oil and heat until slightly smoky, about 1 minute.

3. Carefully pour in the processed spice mix. Stir until aromatic, about 1 minute. Add in the squid rings.

4. Except for 1 can of coconut milk, add all the ingredients of the flavor base into the pressure cooker. Mix gently.

5. Clamp on the lid. Set the cooker on high pressure for 20 minutes with the quick release option.

6. After the pressure is released, carefully remove the lid. Gently stir. Taste and add more fish sauce, if needed.

7. Add in the shrimps first, then the fish fillets. Pour in the remaining can of coconut milk. Do not stir. Clamp on the lid once more. Set the cooker on low pressure for 5 minutes with the normal release option.

8. Once the pressure is released, carefully scoop out the cooked fish. Place on individual serving plates. This is to ensure that the fish doesn't flake away.

9. Give the contents of the pressure cooker a final stir. Adjust seasoning again, if needed.

10. Divide the stew into 4 equal portions and ladle these out on top of the fish fillets. Serve immediately.

Recipe #54 : Chicken Laksa with Ho-fun Noodles

Preparation Time : 30 minutes
Cooking Time : 27 minutes
Serves:4
Equipment Needed : food processor
Ingredients :

For the spice mix

1 piece lemongrass, root and leaves trimmed, use only the white part, roughly chopped

2 pieces garlic cloves, peeled

1 pieceshallot or red onion, peeled, quartered

1 piece fresh turmeric, thumb-sized, peeled, quartered. You can substitute ginger, or about ½ tsp. turmeric powder.

1 pieces Thai chili, stem removed, halved

2 Tbsp. extra virgin olive oil

1 piece lemon, zested, juiced, discard seeds

For the flavor base

1handful dried rice noodles, thick cut, cooked according to package instructions. Approximately ½ cup noodles per person

¼ pound chicken thigh fillets, skins removed, washed, pat dried

1 Tbsp. good quality fish sauce

1 tsp. Spanish or sweet paprika

¼ tsp. black pepper

1 cup chicken or vegetable broth, or plain water

2 cans coconut milk, divided

Directions:

1. Except for the olive oil, lemon zest and juice, process all the ingredients of the spice mix using a food processor.

2. Set the cooker on high pressure. Pour in the olive oil and heat until slightly smoky, about 1 minute.

3. Carefully pour in the processed spice mix. Stir until aromatic, about 1 minute.

4. Except for 1 can of coconut milk and the cooked noodles, add all the ingredients of the flavor base into the pressure cooker. Mix.

5. Clamp on the lid. Set the cooker on high pressure for 25 minutes with the normal release option.

6. After the pressure is released, carefully remove the lid. Gently stir. Taste and add more fish sauce, if needed.

7. Pour in the remaining can of coconut milk, lemon zest and lemon juice. Put the lid back on and let the stew sit undisturbed for 5 to 10 minutes.

8. Place about ½ cup of noodles into individual serving bowls.

9. Once the pressure is released, carefully ladle as much (or as little) laksa stew on top. Serve immediately.

Recipe #55 : Chicken in Coconut Ginger Sauce

Preparation Time : 30 minutes
Cooking Time : 20 minutes, not including the time frying the chicken
beforehand
Serves: 4
Equipment Needed : frying pan; tongs; paper towels
Ingredients :

For the fried chicken

½ pound chicken thighs, bone in, skin on, washed, pat dried

1 tsp. light soy sauce

1 tsp. dark soy sauce

1 tsp. cumin powder

¼ tsp. black pepper

1 cup all purpose flour, add more if needed

oil enough for shallow frying

For the coconut ginger sauce

1 can coconut milk

1 can chicken or vegetable broth

1 Tbsp. brown sugar

1 tsp. tomato paste

1 piece garlic clove, peeled, crushed

1 piece onion, peeled, quartered

¼ cup ginger, peeled, julienned

1 piece fresh bay leaf, whole, washed

1 piece yellow bell pepper, cored, deseeded, diced

1 piece carrot, end removed, unpeeled, diced

2 pieces bird's eye chili, stems removed, minced

Seasonings

good quality fish sauce, to taste

black pepper, to taste

Directions:

1. To prepare the chicken: marinate the chicken pieces in light soy sauce, dark soy sauce, cumin powder and black pepper for at least 6 hours in the fridge. You can do this step hours before, or up to 24 hours prior to cooking.

2. Add cooking oil into a shallow pan until it fills halfway up. Set the flame to medium high heat.

3. Dredge the chicken pieces in the flour and fry in oil until chicken pieces are golden brown but not cooked through, about 4 to 6 minutes per side. Place the half-cooked chicken pieces on paper towels to drain off the excess oil.

4. Place all the ingredients of the coconut ginger sauce into the pressure cooker. Add in the chicken. Mix gently.

5. Set the cooker on high pressure for 20 minutes, with the normal release option.

6. When the pressure is released, carefully remove the lid. Taste, and adjust seasoning using the fish sauce and the black pepper, but only if needed. Serve warm.

Note: to make this a completely vegan meal, you can substitute thick cubes of squash or sweet potatoes for the chicken. You can cook the vegetables exactly like the chicken to give your dish more texture, or you can simply cook the vegetables in the ginger coconut sauce. The latter technique will give you a curry like dish.

Recipe #56 : Chicken and Cauliflower Stew
Preparation Time : 20 minutes

Cooking Time : 25 to 27 minutes
Serves: 4
Ingredients :

1 Tbsp. extra virgin cooking oil

½ pound chicken thigh fillets, bone in, washed, pat dried

1 head cauliflower, washed, drained, cut into florets

2 cups chicken or vegetable broth

1 piece carrot, top removed, peeled, thinly sliced in decorative patterns like flowers or butterflies

1 cupwhite wine

1 Tbsp. white wine vinegar

salt, to taste

black pepper, to taste

For garnishfresh parsley, roughly chopped

Directions:
1. Set the cooker on high pressure. Pour in the oil until slightly smoky, about 1 minute.

2. Using the sauté or browning option of your pressure cooker, cook the chicken pieces until these have browned on all sides, about 4 to 6 minutes.

3. When the chicken is done, pour in the white wine vinegar and deglaze the pot.

4.Except for the cauliflower, carrots, salt and black pepper, add all the remaining ingredients.

5.Clamp on the lid. Set the pressure on high for 15 minutes with the normal pressure release option.

6.After the pressure is released, add in the vegetables. Season the cooking liquid with salt and black pepper.

7.Clamp on the lid once more. Set the pressure on high for 5 minutes with the quick pressure release option.

8.After the pressure is released, check to see if most of the liquid has evaporated. If not, turn on the boil or sauté function of the pressure cooker, and cook until liquid is reduced by half.

9.Once done, divide the stew into 4 equal portions. Ladle into plates. Sprinkle with chopped parsley, if desired. Serve immediately.

Note: you can substitute grated cheese for the parsley, to make this dish more palatable to children.

Conclusion

I am extremely excited to pass this information along to you, and I am so happy that you now have read and can hopefully implement these strategies going forward.

I hope this book was able to help you understand the basics of using a pressure cooker and how to use this when making your daily meals.

The next step is to get started using this information and to hopefully live a healthier but flavorful life!

Please don't be someone who just reads this information and doesn't apply it, the tips and recipes in this book will only benefit you if you use them!

www.ingramcontent.com/pod-product-compliance
Lightning Source LLC
Chambersburg PA
CBHW071438070526
44578CB00001B/125